MW00398517

Killer Kids
Volume Five

22 Shocking
True Murder Cases

Robert Keller

Please Leave Your Review of This Book At
http://bit.ly/kellerbooks

ISBN: 9781712816417

© 2019 by Robert Keller

robertkellerauthor.com

All rights reserved.

No part of this publication may be copied or reproduced in any format, electronic or otherwise, without the prior, written consent of the copyright holder and publisher. This book is for informational and entertainment purposes only and the author and publisher will not be held responsible for the misuse of information contain herein, whether deliberate or incidental.

Much research, from a variety of sources, has gone into the compilation of this material. To the best knowledge of the author and publisher, the material contained herein is factually correct. Neither the publisher, nor author will be held responsible for any inaccuracies.

Table of Contents

Robert Keller

Chris Churchill

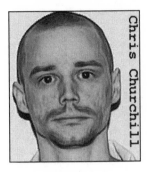

The young man sitting at the defense table, the teenager with the scruffy beard and scraggly mustache, brought his hands up to his head and covered his ears. He could not bear to listen to the words that were being said, couldn't stand the sound of his own voice droning from the television set that was replaying his confession to the members of the jury. In that confession, Chris Churchill was casually recounting the details of five murders, committed a year earlier, when he was just 16 years of age.

Christopher Churchill was born in Illinois in December 1981 and was raised by his mother in the tiny village of Noble, set among the cornfields and oil wells in the southern part of the state. Noble is a peaceful community of just 800 souls, a place where doors were left unlocked and neighbors greeted each other on the street. Unfortunately, Chris Churchill would grow up to be one of its less peaceable residents. By his mid-teens, he had a juvenile record and was known at the local high school for his unruly, anti-social behavior. In 1997, he'd been ejected from the school and transferred to another in nearby Olney. But he remained there less than a month before dropping out later that year. At that time, he was in trouble again, this time for hurling a rock at his girlfriend's mother, hitting her in the eye.

Charges were still pending in that case in the summer of 1997, when there was a surprise arrival in Noble. Jonathan Lloyd was Chris Churchill's half-brother and had moved from Texas where he'd been living with his foster family. He'd relocated to Illinois so that he could get to know his biological mother, Susan, and his brother, Chris. Jonathan was just a year older than Chris but a much calmer and more mature individual. Their mother was hoping that some of that attitude would rub off on her troubled younger son.

In October 1997, there was another set of arrivals in Noble. Debra Smith and her three children, Jennifer, 12; Korey, 10; and Kenny, 6. Debra was a co-worker of Susan, Chris and Jonathan's mom, at a VCR packaging plant. She had recently separated from her husband and had decided to move from Olney to Noble. On arriving in the town, she lived for a short while with Susan, and it was there that she met Jonathan Lloyd. Debra was 32, Jonathan just 17, but the sparks immediately flew between them. They were soon involved in a relationship and had moved in together, renting a single-story frame house on North Noble Avenue. Chris Churchill would quickly become a regular visitor at the home, sometimes staying over.

One such occasion was the evening of Sunday, February 8, 1998. Earlier that day, Jonathan had presented Debra with an engagement ring and she had said yes. The family had also been shopping at Walmart, and the kids had come home bearing gifts, including a bicycle for Korey. Everyone was in high spirits when they arrived at the family residence and found Chris waiting on the doorstep. They

welcomed him in and invited him to share in their evening meal. Then
Chris, Debra, and Jonathan, along with Jennifer, sat down to play a
few hands of cards. It was at this point that Chris's surly side began to
emerge. He became noticeably annoyed after losing consecutive hands
and even more angry when Jonathan and Debra gently teased him over
his abilities as a card player. He was still fuming when the family
retired to bed.

What happened next in the Smith/Lloyd household is the stuff of
nightmares. Angry over what he perceived as his brother's humiliation
of him, Chris sat seething in front of the television, staring blankly at
the screen while he consumed beer after beer. Finally, he decided that
the jibes could not go unanswered. Getting up from his chair, he went
to the kitchen and began rooting around, eventually finding a hammer
under the sink. This he carried to the room shared by 10-year-old
Korey and six-year-old Kenny. Neither of the boys stirred as Churchill
entered. Korey, no doubt dreaming about riding his new bicycle, was
struck first, five vicious blows that shattered his skull and demolished
the brain underneath. Then Churchill turned his attention to the six-
year-old, killing the little boy with an equally vicious onslaught.

Having committed this savage double murder, Churchill returned
calmly to his chair in the lounge. He looked at the clock which showed
5:56. The rest of the family would be rising soon. They, too, would
have to die. A short while later came the sound of an alarm and
Jennifer rising. Having stayed at the house before, Churchill knew her
routine. She'd be heading to her brothers' bedroom to wake them for
school. On this particular morning, she would not make it. Churchill
ambushed her in the passage, striking her down before she was able to
utter a word. Then he headed for the master bedroom where he killed
his brother and Debra Smith in their sleep. Finally, in an act of utter

depravity, he returned to Jennifer and raped the little girl as she lay
dying.

Chris Churchill, a boy of just 16, had brutally slain five people, three
of them children. So what did the juvenile killer do? Did he flee the
scene? Did he try to cover up his crimes? Did he suffer a breakdown?
Did he call the police and give himself up? No, Chris did none of these
things. Instead, he sat for a while watching TV before going to the
bathroom to clean himself up, stepping over Jennifer's corpse on the
way. Then he fixed himself a meal and ate heartily. Finally, he raided
his dead brother's wallet, pocketing nearly $900 in cash. Only then did
he leave the death house.

Over the next six days, Churchill would be seen entering and leaving
the house on several occasions. At the same time, he was flashing the
cash, splurging on takeaway meals, DVDs and other items. When a
friend asked about the source of his newfound wealth, Churchill
casually told him that he'd murdered his brother, his brother's
girlfriend, and "her brats." The teenager laughed it off at the time but,
on later reflection, he wondered whether Churchill might have been
telling the truth. If anyone in their circle was capable of murder, it was
Chris Churchill. Eventually, the friend decided to call the police and
tell them about the conversation. That was how the murders were
uncovered.

Taken into custody, Chris Churchill made no pretense at innocence. In
a videotaped interview (the same interview that he'd later try to block
out in court), he confessed in detail to the crimes. According to
Churchill, he had committed the murders in order to relieve "pent-up
stress." He'd been thinking about killing Jonathan for some time, he

said. The catalyst had been the humiliation he'd suffered at the card table. He also admitted to sexually assaulting Jennifer, saying that he "wanted to do something really bad." If that was his intent, he had surpassed it.

Christopher Churchill was brought to trial in early 1999. Tried as an adult, he was looking at life in prison without parole should he be found guilty. And with his videotaped confession allowed into evidence, it seemed a foregone conclusion that he would be convicted. Churchill's lawyer, William Hoffeditz, had other ideas, however. Hoffeditz launched an inventive defense. He suggested that it was not his client who had committed the murders but a group of his client's friends. Churchill, he claimed, was taking the rap on their behalf out of some misguided sense of loyalty.

It was an interesting hypothesis. Unfortunately for Hoffeditz (and for his client), it was not supported by the evidence, the most damning of which was a Marilyn Manson T-shirt that Churchill admitted wearing at the time of the murders. The shirt had since been washed, but traces of blood were found on the stitching of a sleeve. Subjected to DNA analysis, it returned a match – to Debra Smith.

Convicted on five counts of first-degree murder, Chris Churchill was sentenced to life in prison without parole on May 3, 1999. A subsequent Supreme Court ruling means that he may one day become eligible for release. For now, though, the five-time killer remains securely behind bars.

Heather Smith

We all remember our first love, the intensity of it, the passion that our teenaged brains are not yet fully equipped to comprehend. We remember also the flip side of the coin, the dark side, that first, devastating breakup. It feels like our whole world has come to an end, like we will never recover from the heartbreak. And yet, the vast majority of us do recover, and move on, and love again. And even if, in later years, we cast a nostalgic eye back on those halcyon days, we realize that it was all just a dress rehearsal for the real thing, the lives that we eventually carve out for ourselves.

Not so with 14-year-old Heather Smith. A talented and pretty girl, Heather was a straight-A student and a member of the Honor Society at Spanaway Junior High School in Spanaway, Washington. She often helped out as a teacher's aide and was also on the school gymnastics team. Classmates and teachers described her as pleasant but driven, a go-getter who set high standards for herself and seldom fell short of these self-imposed benchmarks.

But in the fall of 1985, those in Heather's circle noticed a troubling change in her demeanor. The once-bubbly teen had become decidedly downbeat, depressed even. She once confided in a friend that she was contemplating suicide and showed her a scar on her wrist where she'd cut herself. Her academic performance started to suffer as she turned in the first B of her high school career. She even spoke of bringing a gun to school and shooting her ex-boyfriend, 15-year-old Gordon Pickett.

Of course, none of Heather's friends took this latter threat seriously, although perhaps they should have. Heather's depression, after all, had coincided directly with Gordon calling an end to their relationship, saying that things between them were getting too serious. He'd asked if they could downgrade their relationship to a friendship, and Heather had, at first, agreed.

However, it was soon apparent that Heather was taking the breakup badly. She started stalking Gordon and even threatened him with violence, an episode that saw both of them called into the guidance counselor's office for a sit-down. There, they agreed to a truce, but then two events occurred that would shatter the agreement. First, Heather discovered that Gordon was dating another girl. Then she found out that she was pregnant. It was at that point that Heather finally reached the depths of her despair, at that point that she decided on a truly dreadful way out of her predicament.

Tuesday, November 26, 1985, was an ordinary day at Spanaway High. When school let out at 3 p.m., most of the students headed home while others stayed behind for extra-curricular activities. Heather Smith was among the former, while Gordon Pickett headed for the gym. He was on the school wrestling team and planned on getting in some extra practice with his friend and teammate, Chris Ricco. Soon the pair of them would be out on the mat, running through some moves.

Heather, meanwhile, had traveled the short distance to her family home where she now sat on the edge of her bed, stewing over her situation. She knew what needed to be done and yet, even now, she wondered if she could go through with it. But this is where Heather's innate sense of purpose kicked in. When something needed to be done, she got it done. That was ingrained in her character. Getting up from her bed, she walked briskly to her parents' bedroom. She rummaged through her father's closet, retrieving the .22-caliber semi-automatic rifle that was kept there. After checking that the weapon was loaded, she carried it back to her bedroom. There, she pulled on her coat and concealed the rifle under it. A short while later, she knocked on her neighbor's door and asked for a lift to school, claiming that she'd left an important homework assignment behind.

Arriving at the school, Heather walked directly toward the gymnasium, where she removed the rifle from her coat and sat down on a bench in the snow-covered lot outside the building. Her plan was to wait until Gordon emerged, but she soon grew impatient and asked Matthew Hone, a student who she saw heading towards the gym, to send Gordon out to talk to her. Spotting the rifle leaning up against the bench beside her, Hone was somewhat skeptical. "What are you going to do with that?" he asked. "Blow his brains out?" To that, Heather just chuckled.

"I don't even know how to load this thing," she said. It was at that moment that Gordon Pickett and Chris Ricco emerged from the gym.

Heather wasted no time on formalities. Without saying a word, she snatched up the rifle, shouldered it, and aimed at her former boyfriend. Aware of what was about to happen, Chris bravely stepped in front of his friend. But if he thought that Heather would hesitate to shoot him, too, he was tragically mistaken. She unleashed a hail of bullets, hitting both Chris and Gordon several times in the chest and in the head. The boys collapsed into the snow, staining it with their blood. Heather then walked calmly away while Matthew, somewhat less composed, sprinted toward the school building.

When police and paramedics arrived on the scene a short while later, Heather was nowhere to be found. By then, Gordon Pickett was already dead and Chris Ricco was in critical condition. He was rushed to Madigan Army Medical Center but would die later that night, despite the best efforts of doctors.

For now, though, the police had another problem on their hands, an obviously disturbed young girl, wandering the streets with a semi-automatic rifle. An immediate search was launched for Heather Smith, who had been identified to police by Matthew Hone. However, Heather somehow managed to avoid her pursuers for several hours, until she walked back onto the school grounds, still carrying the rifle.

With the grounds now crawling with officers, including a SWAT team, it is uncertain why Heather returned there. Perhaps it was to give herself up. If that was the case, she apparently had a change of heart at the last moment. As police officers surrounded her and ordered her to put the gun down, Heather responded with a shrill, "No, I won't!" Then, before anyone could intervene, she put the rifle barrel to her head and pulled the trigger. As she collapsed to the ground, medics immediately rushed in to provide assistance. It was too late. Heather Smith, fatally wounded, died on the way to hospital.

Daphne Abdela & Christopher Vasquez

Daphne Abdela had endured a tragic start to life. When she was still a toddler, both of her parents were killed in an auto wreck, leaving her all alone in the world and confined to the care of the New York State Office of Children and Family Services. It was a terrible tragedy, of course, but it was one that would at least have a happy ending. The little orphan was adopted by a wealthy New York couple. Angelo Abdela was an executive with a major international food conglomerate; his wife, Catherine, was a French-born former fashion model. They lived in a swish Central Park West apartment, took vacations abroad, ate in the finest restaurants. Daphne might not have realized it yet, but she had been thrust into a life of luxury and privilege. She would grow up attending exclusive private schools and having her every need catered to.

But, as Angelo and Catherine were to discover, the little girl that they'd brought into their lives was no angel. Daphne might have looked like butter wouldn't melt in her mouth, but that baby-faced expression of wide-eyed innocence was a lie. Behind the façade, something else was lurking, something dangerous. Daphne grew to be a belligerent child, one who regarded her adoptive parents with barely concealed loathing. She frequently directed verbal abuse at them and, on more than one occasion, attacked them physically. In fact, the abuse got so bad that Angelo took out a restraining order against his daughter. Eventually, he and Catherine just gave up and let Daphne do whatever she pleased. That usually involved rollerblading in Central Park and getting drunk. By the time she was 15 years old, Daphne had already been diagnosed as an alcoholic and was attending AA meetings. It was also around that time that she met Christopher Vasquez.

Christopher's upbringing had been quite different to Daphne's. His family lived in a tiny fourth-story walk-up where Christopher spent most of his days indoors, a hangover of the agoraphobia he'd suffered as a child. At 15, he was a nerdy kid, studious, bespectacled and decidedly uncool in his polo shirts and bad haircut. He was also on anxiety medication and had been diagnosed with clinical depression. Desperate to fit in, Christopher often spoke of joining a gang. He even started hanging around with some local toughs, although he was always on the fringes, never really accepted. That was how it had always been for Christopher until the day that Daphne Abdela came rollerblading into his life.

Daphne was smart, she was pretty, and she talked tough, all of which made a big impression on Christopher. He wanted desperately to be her boyfriend, and she sometimes strung him along, making him believe that he was. At times, she'd be all over Christopher, showering him with faux affection. Then she'd push him away, ignore him altogether, openly flirt with other boys and even adult men. One can only imagine the effect this must have had on a teenager already suffering with anxiety issues. In the group of delinquents that he and Daphne hung around with, everyone could see what was going on.

None of them would speak out against Daphne, though. They were all too afraid of her.

And so to the evening of May 22, 1997. Daphne and Christopher were in Central Park that night, hanging with friends, drinking, smoking, and rollerblading the paths. Daphne was also engaging in her favorite pastime, talking tough and boasting that she was going to commit a murder. The group had heard it all before. Daphne loved to brag about what a badass she was, so when she pulled a switchblade and said that she planned to "slice someone" that night, nobody took her seriously – no one but Christopher Vasquez. He too was carrying a knife, one that he showed to Daphne once the rest of the group had drifted away. Perhaps he saw this as an opportunity to impress his girlfriend, perhaps it was bravado garnered from the bottle. Either way, he told Daphne that he wanted to help her. Daphne seemed thrilled at the prospect. By moonlight, to the chirping of insects and the faint thrum of New York traffic, they set off, hunting for a victim.

Michael McMorrow was a forty-something Manhattan real estate agent who lived close to the park and was a regular visitor. He enjoyed hanging out in Strawberry Fields, where he sometimes participated in an ad hoc storytelling group. That was where Daphne and Christopher found him that night. McMorrow was known to Daphne Abdela. They had been in alcohol rehab together. "Hey, Irish," she said, when she spotted him. "Want to go down to the lake with me and Chris and drink some beer?" McMorrow said that he would, just as soon as he was finished telling his story. Abdela and Vasquez then hung around for a while, waiting until McMorrow was done. Eventually, the three of them left, walking together towards Central Park Lake. That was the last time that anyone, bar his killers, saw Michael McMorrow alive.

What happened at the lake that night would become a matter of much conjecture at the trial to follow, with Abdela and Vasquez each accusing the other of initiating the attack and of being the main aggressor. What the police were able to determine is that the threesome sat drinking beer for a while before Abdela and Vasquez drew their knives and started threatening McMorrow.

At first, McMorrow thought that they were just kidding around. But he quickly appreciated the gravity of the situation once he was cut for the first time. Then he tried to fight back but, despite being bigger and heavier than his attackers, he was outnumbered. He was also unarmed, and he'd been drinking, making him unsteady on the uneven ground. Still, he managed to keep them at bay until Daphne swept his feet from under him, sending him crashing to the ground. Then Vasquez was on him, slashing and stabbing in a frenzied attack. "Cut him!" Daphne screamed as McMorrow begged for mercy, "Slice him from ear to ear!" If it was mercy that McMorrow was expecting, he found none. Suffering from multiple wounds, his face and throat slashed, his lungs collapsed, his nose and wrist almost severed, Michael McMorrow eventually bled out on the ground.

Yet even now, Daphne Abdela's bloodlust was not sated. She ordered Vasquez to remove McMorrow's shirt and to gut him so that he'd sink when they threw him into the lake. Vasquez, as always, complied, burying the blade in McMorrow's belly and hacking upward, opening a gaping wound that left the intestines exposed. Then he helped his girlfriend force rocks into their victim's abdominal cavity before dragging the body into the shallows where it soon disappeared below the water. That done, the two young killers walked away, heading for Daphne's apartment building where they planned to clean up.

But, unbeknownst to Daphne, an alarm had already been raised with the police. Angelo Adbela had become concerned when his daughter was several hours past her curfew. He'd phoned the police and reported her missing. By the time that Daphne and Christopher arrived, a patrol car was parked outside. Unperturbed, Daphne led Christopher into a basement laundry room where they stripped down and started washing the blood from their bodies.

While all of this was going on, the police had started a search of the building and had been informed by a neighbor that he'd seen two kids sneaking into the basement. Daphne and Christopher were caught in the act, half-naked and with blood on their hands. Asked where the blood had come from, Daphne quickly explained that they had fallen while rollerblading. Small cuts and nicks on their hands and arms seemed to back them up, and so the officers accepted the story and left.

But now Daphne was worried. Despite their efforts to conceal the body, she felt sure that Michael McMorrow would be found soon and that the police would link the murder to her. After all, it was she who had invited McMorrow down to the lake. Better to go on the offensive rather than waiting for the cops to come to her. She therefore called in an anonymous tip to the NYPD, telling them about a body sunk to the depths of Central Park Lake. Unfortunately for her, the police were able to run a trace on the call. Soon detectives were knocking on the door and Daphne was telling them what she knew about the murder. Despite her father's admonishment not to say anything without a lawyer, she immediately started talking, putting the blame squarely on Christopher Vasquez.

According to Daphne, the murder had been committed out of jealousy. She said that Christopher Vasquez thought that he was her boyfriend and had totally "lost it" after he'd seen her and Michael McMorrow kissing. He'd then attacked McMorrow and stabbed him to death. She admitted that she'd help dispose of the corpse but denied participating in the actual killing. Later, she'd lead the police to the spot where the body had been submerged. As McMorrow was brought to the surface, she started shouting: "I tried to help you! I tried to give you CPR!" Given the severe mutilations that had been inflicted on the corpse, CPR would have been like applying a Band-Aid to an amputation.

Daphne was adamant that her story of how Michael McMorrow had died was the truth. Unfortunately for her, the District Attorney was not convinced by her professed innocence. Both she and Vasquez were arrested and charged with manslaughter, a controversial move which the D.A. would later explain to the media. According to him, no jury would have convicted the young killers of murder; no one would have wanted to believe that two teenagers could have willfully inflicted such horrific damage.

At trial, the Abdelas predictably brought in a heavy hitter to represent their daughter. Ben Brafman was one of New York's toughest defense attorneys. Christopher Vasquez had to be satisfied with less celebrated representation, but the outcome was nonetheless the same. Both defendants were found guilty and sentenced to ten years in prison. They each served six years before being released in January of 2004.

Luke Mitchell

It was the spring of 2003. At St David's High School in Dalkeith, Scotland, 14-year-old Jodi Jones had a new crush. The object of her infatuation was another 14-year-old, her classmate Luke Mitchell. Luke was a bit of a rebel with an air of danger about him. He liked dressing in dark clothing and listening to the music of controversial rock star, Marilyn Manson. He was rumored to be a cannabis dealer and a user of the drug, but that in no way put Jodi off. If anything, it made Luke more interesting, more edgy. When he asked her out in March of that year, she barely skipped a beat before accepting. Soon the two 14-year-olds were involved in a sexual relationship.

It is easy to see what attracted Luke and Jodi to each other. They were from similar backgrounds and lived in the same area; they liked the same music and enjoyed dressing in dark "goth-style" clothing. They were also fond of cannabis, albeit Jodi only indulged sporadically while Luke was a heavy user. The romance, in any case, bloomed. Over the next few months, the teenagers were virtually inseparable. By June 2003, they were seeing each other on most weeknights, and over the weekends. Usually they would rendezvous at one of their houses, which were separated by the half-mile expanse of Roan's Dyke Path, a lane that ran between the neighborhoods of Easthouses, where Jodi lived, and Newbattle, where Luke shared a home with his mother and older brother.

During the last week of June 2003, Jodi Jones was grounded by her mother for missing a curfew. That restriction was finally lifted on the afternoon of June 30 and, of course, Jodi's first call was to her boyfriend. After the pair exchanged texts, Jodi told her mother that she was going to visit Luke. Judith Jones had forbidden her daughter from walking Roan's Dyke Path alone after dark, but since it was not yet dusk, she made no objection. Jodi walked away from her house at 16:50. She would never return.

About 50 minutes later, at 17:40, the phone jangled into life at the Jones residence. Alan Ovens, Judith Jones's boyfriend, answered and was surprised to hear Luke Mitchell's voice on the other end of the line, asking if Jodi was home. Ovens told him that Jodi had left to visit him, and Luke then replied "Okay, cool," and hung up. The call alarmed Ovens enough for him to mention it to Judith. The walk should have taken Jodi no more than 25 minutes. She should have been at Luke's house long ago. Judith, however, did not share her boyfriend's concerns. She figured that Jodi must have met a friend along the way and stopped to chat.

The next significant point in the story occurs at 22:00. Jodi was meant to be home at that time, but she still hadn't returned. Annoyed, her mom waited until 22:40 and then sent a text to Luke, telling him to send Jodi home immediately and to inform her that her grounding had been reinstated. Judith could not have expected the response that she got, a call from Luke telling her that he had not seen Jodi that evening. She had never showed up at his house.

Alarm bells now jangling, Judith quickly assembled her family into a search party. At 23:00, Judith, her older daughter, Janine, Janine's boyfriend, Steven Kelly, and Jodi's grandmother, Alice Walker, set off along Roan's Dyke Path, walking into a strong wind and lashing rain. At the same time, Luke Mitchell was leaving his home in Newbattle, heading down the path from the opposite direction with his dog. He met up with the Jones party near the east end of the lane. Then they all turned around and started walking back in a westerly direction.

Roan's Dyke Path was bounded on one side by a crumbling wall which separated it from the woodland beyond. At one point, the wall had collapsed, forming a sort of "V" which gave access to the woods. It was in this vicinity that Luke Mitchell's dog started acting up, pulling him in the direction of the gap. Stepping through, he found himself in dense foliage. Ducking under the overhanging branches, he turned west and walked along the inside of the wall, led on by the dog. He'd covered only a short distance when he spotted something protruding from the undergrowth. Closer inspection showed it to be a human foot clad in an ankle sock. Jodi Jones had been found.

Jodi was lying on her back on the ground, naked but for her socks. Her hands were bound behind her back with her jeans, while the rest of her clothing lay strewn around the area. She had numerous injuries, including cuts to her right cheek, her left breast, and her stomach. Incisions had also been made around both eyes, later determined to have been inflicted post-mortem. There were also defensive injuries to her hands and arms, suggesting that she had struggled with her assailant. All of these paled, however, compared to the damage to her throat. Here, the killer had used a knife to inflict horrendous damage, slicing through the windpipe, the jugular vein and the carotid artery. She would have bled out in mere minutes. And what was the motive for this horrific crime? The condition of the body suggested strongly that this was sexually motivated. However, the autopsy would later reveal that Jodi had not been penetrated.

From the very start, investigators were suspicious of Luke Mitchell. This was based mainly on the circumstances under which the body had been discovered. How was it possible that Mitchell had found Jodi so quickly, in pitch darkness and in poor weather conditions? Mitchell claimed that it was his dog that had led him to the corpse, saying that the animal had started "acting up" and had virtually pulled him through the gap in the wall. However, others in the impromptu search party disputed this and said that the dog had shown no reaction at all. This would turn out to be the key piece of "evidence" against Luke Mitchell. Despite the best efforts of investigators, there was nothing to link him forensically to the crime. When he was eventually arrested in April 2004, it was based almost entirely on the "guilty knowledge" he possessed regarding the location of the corpse.

Luke Mitchell went on trial at the High Court of Justiciary in Edinburgh in late 2004. He entered a plea of not guilty, offering a defense that was as shaky as the prosecution case against him. According to Mitchell, he had been at home cooking dinner at the time that Jodi was killed. Unfortunately for him, this alibi was contradicted by his brother. In his testimony, Shane Mitchell swore that Luke was not home that night. He knew this, he said, because he was watching internet porn that evening and only ever did so when he was certain that no one else was in the house. This testimony would prove a death blow to the defense. After a 42-day trial, the jury took just five hours to convict Luke Mitchell of murder. He was sentenced to life in prison with a minimum tariff of 20 years. Mitchell would later launch an appeal which was ultimately rejected.

In the years since Luke Mitchell was sent to prison, there has been much debate around the safety of his conviction. Mitchell continues to insist that he did not kill Jodi, and there are many who feel that he was wrongly convicted, that there exists at least a reasonable doubt as to his guilt. But there is one question that neither Mitchell nor his supporters have been able to answer. How did he know the location of Jodi's body? His story that the dog led him there simply does not ring true. There is only one way that he could have known where Jodi was. He put her there himself.

Robert Keller

Anthony Santo

Juvenile serial killers are a rare but not unknown phenomenon, as the infamous cases of Mary Bell, Cayetano Godino, and Jesse Pomeroy attest. There was also Craig Price, a teenage psychopath who stabbed and beat four victims to death before the age of 16. Price is often referenced as the youngest serial killer in American history, but that is only because few people have heard of Anthony Santo. Incredibly, this young killer committed three bloody murders before his fifteenth birthday.

We know very little about Anthony Santo's background, other than the fact that he was born in Italy in 1894 and immigrated to America with his parents as a toddler. The family settled in Brooklyn, New York, where they had relatives already living. Anthony was, by all accounts, a normal, happy child. But then, in 1900, he was struck down by a bout of scarlet fever, leaving him bedridden for several months. He would eventually recover from the disease but, thereafter, it was clear to all who knew him that something was amiss. The boy was prone to erratic behavior. He claimed to hear voices and to experience hallucinations. Most frightening of all, he suffered "mad spells" during which his behavior turned violent.

In1908, Santo was 14 years old and still living in Brooklyn. He had formed a close bond with his cousins, Frank and James Marino, aged 18 and 12 respectively. The boys liked to hang out and play games in the woods near 6th Street. But then one day early in March, Santo emerged from the woods alone, claiming amnesia and saying that he did not know what had become of his cousins. A search was then launched but turned up no sign of the youngsters. It was feared that they might have come to harm, but there were also suggestions that they might have run away from home. In any case, the police did not expend a huge amount of resources looking for them. Frank was already of age, and it was believed that James was probably with him and under his care.

Not long after the disappearance of the Marino brothers, Anthony Santo received an offer of a job in Boston. A cousin was working on the construction of the new sewage works there and had arranged a position for him. Since there were limited opportunities for a boy of low intelligence and no schooling, Anthony's parents allowed him to go. In truth, they may have been relieved to have him off their hands.

Shortly after Santo started his new job, there was a horrific murder close to where he was lodging. Six-year-old Louise Staula had gone missing, and a police search turned up her body in a meadow beside the Charles River. The cause of death was unusual. It appeared that the little girl had been stoned to death, like some biblical apostate. Ten fist-sized rocks were found near the body, and several were bloodstained. It appeared that the killer had hurled the missiles at the child, hitting her on the head and causing massive brain injuries.

While the police were still puzzling over this unusual murder, a seemingly unrelated crime was being reported in East Boston, this one a far more trivial affair involving the theft of a bicycle. It was solved on June 6, 1908, when a beat cop spotted 14-year-old Anthony Santo pedaling around on the stolen cycle. Santo was arrested on the spot and taken to the lockup at the nearest police station. There he astonished his captors by saying that he wanted to confess to murder.

Once Santo started talking, it was clear which murder he was referring to. He was claiming responsibility for killing Louise Staula.

According to Santo's confession, he had been walking through Dedham on the afternoon of May 11 when he spotted Louise playing alone in a meadow. On seeing the little girl, a "mad spell" came over him, and he picked up a handful of rocks and started hurling them at her. Louise tried to run, but she was struck on the head and collapsed into the long grass. Santo then caught up with her and finished the job with a few well-aimed stones. Then the "spell" was lifted and, realizing what he'd done, Santo started praying to God to "make her get better." Eventually, however, he realized that Louise must already be dead. He then fled the scene, leaving the body behind.

The details that Santo had given left the police in no doubt that he was telling the truth. But he wasn't done yet. He still had two more murders to confess, these committed in New York. The victims in this case were his cousins, Frank and James Marino. Santo said that on a day in March 1908 (he couldn't remember the exact date), he, Frank and James had entered the 6th Street woods together, as they often did. On this day, however, he'd been overcome by one of his "mad spells" and had picked up some rocks and started throwing them at his cousins. Both boys were struck, in James's case fatally. Frank, meanwhile, was lying on the ground, injured and moaning in pain. Santo put him out of his misery by drawing his pocket knife and stabbing him to death. He then buried the bodies, although he couldn't recall where the makeshift graves were located. There was enough about the story, though, to suggest that it was true. Many of the details would later be confirmed by the NYPD.

Anthony Santo was now in serious trouble, facing trial for a child murder in Massachusetts before possible extradition to New York to face charges there. But Santo would never see the inside of a courtroom. It was clear that all was not right with the boy, and this was confirmed when he was examined by a team of doctors. They declared him "feeble-minded," delusional, and suffering from hallucinations. Unfit, therefore, to stand trial.

Anthony Santo was ordered to be confined indefinitely to the State Lunatic Hospital in Taunton, Massachusetts (now known as Taunton State Hospital). He is believed to have died there, although the date and cause of death are not known.

Jacquiline "Nikki" Reynolds

Just after 7 p.m. on the evening of May 14, 1997, a 911 dispatcher in Broward County, Florida, received a particularly disturbing call. On the line was a hysterical young woman who said that she had just murdered her mother. Units were then dispatched to the address the caller gave, arriving at the neat Coral Springs bungalow to find 17-year-old Nikki Reynolds standing on the doorstep, covered in blood.

And the scene inside the house was even worse. Billie Jean Reynolds was lying on the floor in the living room in a pool of her own blood, some of which had left a trail behind her as she'd tried to drag herself to safety. She was still breathing, and paramedics acted quickly to apply emergency medical treatment while wheeling her to the waiting ambulance. She was then rushed to Broward North Medical Center. In the meanwhile, her daughter was loaded into a police car. "Please God, let her live, please let her live…" Nikki Reynolds repeated over and over again as she sat in the back of the cruiser. Those prayers, however, would go unanswered. Billie Jean Reynolds was D.O.A. at the hospital. The blood loss from 25 knife wounds had been just too much.

But how had it come to this? How had a respectful, churchgoing teenager ended up brutally stabbing her mother to death? To answer that, we have to go back to 1979, the year that Jaquiline Nicole Reynolds was born. Billie Jean Reynolds and her husband Robert were not Nikki's biological parents. They adopted her at three months, after her mother had given her up. And, in the manner of most adoptive parents, they absolutely doted on the child. Nikki had every advantage growing up, and she rewarded her parents by being a sweet and soft-spoken girl, academically gifted at school, active with her mom and dad in the Coral Springs Baptist Church. However, there was a dark side to Nikki, one that was perhaps the fault of Robert and Billie Jean. They seldom denied their daughter anything. If they did, she'd throw a tantrum. In short, the Reynoldses had raised a spoiled brat.

Temper tantrums, however, would prove to be the least of her parents' problems once Nikki hit puberty. At 16, she began dating a high school classmate named Carlos Infante and became sexually active with him. Robert and Billie Jean knew nothing of this until an incident in 1996, when Nikki claimed to have been raped. The police were called, of course, but Nikki's story quickly fell apart under questioning. She eventually admitted that she'd made up the rape to conceal the fact that she was pregnant by Carlos. That, too, would turn out to be a lie. She wasn't pregnant at all. But for Nikki's parents, it was nonetheless devastating. Their little girl was sexually active. It went against their Christian beliefs and everything they stood for.

In the aftermath of the rape allegations, relations between Nikki and her parents, especially her mother, took a significant downturn. Mother and daughter were often involved in arguments that all too frequently devolved into screaming matches. Nikki was repeatedly grounded but would defy her parents by climbing out of her bedroom window and sneaking off to see Carlos. In the meantime, Nikki's academic performance had plummeted. Previously, she'd been a solid A student. Now her report card was littered with F's. Matters finally came to a head on May 13, 1997, when Billie Jean got a call from her daughter's high school counselor, asking her and her husband to come to the school for a meeting the following morning.

The news that the counselor had to share was another body blow to Billie Jean and Robert. Nikki had confided that she was pregnant with Carlos Infante's child. But was she really? Given Nikki's history of lies on the issue, Billie Jean took her straight from the school to a pharmacy, where she bought a pregnancy testing kit. The results of the test were negative. Nikki had been lying again, infuriating her mother.

And it wasn't just Billie Jean who was mad at the deception. Carlos Infante was angry, too. His relationship with Nikki had been a rocky one. Carlos found his girlfriend to be clingy and overbearing. Several times he'd tried to break up with her, and each time she'd convinced him to stay with the same story, claiming that she was pregnant. Well, this time, Carlos had had enough. When he spoke to Nikki later that day, he told her that it was over. Nikki's response was to go into the bathroom and swallow a fistful of aspirin.

The drama that had started with a flawed teenage romance and would end in a bloody murder was now approaching its endgame. The school counselor had asked Billie Jean and Robert to bring Nikki back for a follow-up meeting the next day, but Billie Jean was not convinced that it would do much good. As with most things in life, she believed that the answer lay in her faith, and she therefore told Nikki that she was taking her to the church to speak to one of the counselors there. Nikki, already woozy from the pills she'd taken, didn't argue. However, the meeting was a disaster, with Nikki and the counselor getting into a shouting match before the teenager stormed out.

Later, back at the Reynolds residence, things were tense as the family sat down to dinner. Nikki, still depressed over her last conversation with Carlos, was sullen, brooding. In her brain, a plan was fermenting, one that involved killing the boy who had abandoned her. She could imagine waiting for Carlos in the school hall, waiting until his first class let out. Then she'd step up behind him, grab him by the hair and draw a knife across his throat. That would teach him. The more she thought about it, the more she believed that she could actually go through with it, that she could actually murder her boyfriend.

But then Nikki realized that there was a problem with her plan. She was due to attend a meeting with the guidance counselor the next morning. She wouldn't be there to kill Carlos. Her next thought was a massive escalation of her original idea. What if she were to kill her parents, too? Then she could skip the counseling session and be waiting for Carlos when he emerged from class. In her drug-addled brain, this outlandish idea quickly solidified into the only way out of her current predicament.

It is at this point that the story takes yet another twist. Nikki had thought that her parents would be staying in that night, but now Robert announced that he was going to the church for a few hours. He asked Billie Jean to go with him, but she declined, saying that she wanted to do some work on her computer. Robert then left the house and Billie

Jean sent Nikki to do the dishes while she took her laptop and went into the living room.

This turn of events was a blow to Nikki, who now thought that she would have to abandon her plan. But standing over the sink full of dishes, she suddenly had an epiphany. This actually made things easier. Now she could kill her mother, hide the body, and then wait for her father to come home before killing him, too. A large kitchen knife sat on the counter. Nikki picked it up and ran the edge of the blade along her thumb to test its sharpness. Then she got a grip on the handle and walked towards the living room where Billie Jean was typing away at her computer.

Nikki Reynolds was one of the most cooperative murder suspects that the Coral Springs Police Department had ever had. Not only did she confess to the murder, she provided a graphic blow-by-blow account of what had happened. Some of the content was extremely disturbing. She said that she'd come up behind her mother and had tried to cut her throat. But the knife had not even broken skin, and Billie Jean had jumped to her feet and asked what she was doing. It was at this point that Nikki launched her attack, continuing the onslaught even after her mother collapsed to the floor. At one point, she'd asked, "Are you dying yet?" and Billie Jean replied that she thought she was, that she felt her spirit slipping away. Nikki then stabbed her "three or four" more times because she didn't want her to "suffer unnecessarily."

By the time the matter came to trial in 1999, the battle lines had been clearly drawn. The prosecution was calling it premeditated murder and was asking for life in prison; the defense was seeking a verdict of not guilty by reason of insanity. This was based on two things – a diagnosis of borderline personality disorder, and Nikki's attempted overdose on the day of the murder. Aspirin, according to the experts, can cause a psychotic episode if taken in excess.

This was a complex case, one that the initial jury was unable to adjudicate. With jurors deadlocked at six to six, the judge had no option but to declare a mistrial. The second jury would prove more decisive, finding Nikki Reynolds guilty of second-degree murder. She was sentenced to 34 years in prison, although that was reduced to 21 years on appeal. Nikki Reynolds is currently incarcerated at Gadsden Correctional Facility in Quincy, Florida.

James Osmanson

James Osmanson was ten years old and already he had endured more turmoil in his young life than most people see in the entirety of theirs. First his parents, Robert and Cindy, were both diagnosed with AIDS. Then they divorced, with Cindy gaining custody of James. A short while later, she remarried and moved with her new husband, Billy Trimbach, to Colorado, where the next traumatic event in young James's life would occur. On February 14, 1993, Billy Trimbach's body was found beside a rural road in Weld County, Colorado.

Billy had been shot to death, dragged to the side of the road and dumped among the weeds. Subsequent investigation showed that Cindy had taken out a large insurance policy on his life just weeks before he was killed. That made her a suspect, and the police soon had even more compelling evidence that this was a murder-for-profit. Billy's signature on the policy turned out to be a forgery. And something else did not sit well with investigators, the statement given by Cindy's nine-year-old son James. The boy swore that he'd seen his stepfather drive away with a strange man on the night he was killed. Detectives believed he was lying, probably under instruction from his mother. Before they could get around to questioning him further, however, Cindy Trimbach was gone. She'd packed up her kids and her belongings and moved to Butte, Montana.

Cindy may have hoped for a fresh start in her new hometown, but for James, the move would turn out to be a disaster. Enrolled at the Margaret Leary Elementary School, he soon became a target for bullies. Then one of the kids found out that James's mother had AIDS, and from that point on, his life became a living hell. He was constantly taunted, not just at school but by kids who lived in his neighborhood, too. And the jibes were ugly, focusing on his mother's sex life and on her imminent death. Children can be incredibly cruel. To a ten-year-old kid who loved his mother and could not understand why others would want to say such mean things about her, it must have been unbearable.

And so James decided to do something about it. His mother had a .22-caliber pistol that she kept somewhat carelessly around the house. On the morning of April 12, 1994, James took the gun and stored it in his book bag. All of that day at school, he carried it around with him, weighing heavy in the bag. He knew what he wanted to do. All he needed was the right moment. It came that afternoon after classes had finished for the day and students were streaming through the school gates. Walking among the throng, James spotted his nemesis up ahead, his most spiteful tormentor, the kid who never let up, never missed a chance to pass some hurtful jibe. On any other day, James would have slunk away, praying that he would not be seen. Not today.

"Hey, AIDS baby!" the bully yelled as he spotted James among the mass of kids, "How's your mom doing?" He was wearing that look that James so hated, that cruel, glint-eyed grin. But the look faded instantly when James reached into his bag and his hand came out holding the gun. Then the bully's faced blanched white, and he threw his arm up to his face in a vain attempt to protect himself.

Three shots were pulled off in quick succession, each one of them missing its target. One passed through a student's coat without injuring the child; a second was later found inside another student's backpack; the third, tragically, struck an unintended target. Eleven-year-old

Jeremy Bullock had never participated in the bullying of James Osmanson, but it was he who would pay the price. The third bullet struck him in the head, inflicting a mortal wound.

Jeremy Bullock died in hospital the next day. There was never any doubt as to who had pulled the trigger, and James Osmanson did not deny culpability. Still, there was no possibility that he would be charged with murder. His age precluded him from prosecution in the state of Montana. Instead, a judge ordered that he be sent for psychiatric evaluation. Thereafter, he would be placed with foster parents who were both trained counselors. He would continue to receive therapy until the age of 18 when his probationary period would come to an end. It was a sensible response to a tragic event and one supported by the victim's family. "There is no doubt that a ten-year-old who commits this type of act needs a lot of help and support and treatment," said Robin Bullock, Jeremy's mother. "I don't think you can ever lock away a child without support because he's not going to get better on his own."

Of course, the Bullock family had trauma of its own to process, as did the staff and students of Margaret Leary Elementary and the broader community of Butte. Such events simply did not happen in rural Montana. As one commentator put it, "this was big city stuff." In the days following the shooting, trained counselors were brought in from across the state to talk to traumatized kids. Meanwhile, the Bullock family was inundated with hundreds of letters and cards of condolence and support. So many people attended Jeremy's funeral that events from inside the church had to be projected onto a television screen for those watching outside. At the funeral, plans were announced for a soccer field which would be named in Jeremy's memory. The Jeremy Bullock Memorial Soccer Field has since grown into an entire sports complex. It was a fitting tribute for an innocent little boy who had been so tragically taken.

As for the other little boy at the center of these events, his tribulations were far from over. In the two years that followed the shooting, both of James Osmanson's parents died of AIDS. A few years later, his older brother, Kevin, hanged himself while serving time at the Montana State Prison. Death, it seemed, had taken up residence in his life and was refusing to be shifted.

But children can be remarkably resilient in the face of tragedy, and James Osmanson was more resilient than most. Placed under the legal guardianship of Butte lawyer, Brad Belke, James did well in foster care. He was an intelligent child who became an avid reader and a skilled chess player. He did well at school and eventually graduated. At age 18, his probationary period ended, and he got an apartment and a job as he prepared to attend college. During all that time, he never gave his foster parents a moment of trouble. "We did the best we could for James and he turned his life around," Brad Belke said. It was a remarkable tale of redemption.

Don Steenkamp

It was just after dusk on Good Friday, April 6, 2012. In the small town of Griekwastad in South Africa's Northern Cape province, traffic was sparse on the streets. The town is not exactly renowned for its nightlife. Then, out of the gloom, an Isuzu pickup emerged, traveling at high speed. Those who saw the vehicle pass, recognized it. It belonged to a wealthy local farmer named Deon Steenkamp. It wasn't Steenkamp at the wheel, though; it was his 15-year-old son, Don. Now the teenager brought the pickup to a screeching halt in front of the town's only police station. He'd barely done so when he was out of the vehicle and sprinting inside. There, he delivered grim news to the few policemen on duty. His father, mother, and younger sister had all been murdered.

Farm murders are a disquieting feature of modern South African life, with farmers living in constant fear of attack from roving bands of criminals. On an almost weekly basis, there are new reports of atrocities, of rape, torture, and murder, of horrific acts perpetrated against the elderly and even babies. Some have likened it to a genocide, and it doesn't help that the government refuses to acknowledge the problem. Some radical politicians even call it "justified retribution" for the ills of the country's previous apartheid regime.

So when the report came in of a triple homicide at the Steenkamp farm, it was initially assumed that the family had fallen victim to a "farm attack." The police officers who headed out to the crime scene with a blood-spattered Don Steenkamp sitting in the back seat, certainly believed this was what they would find. But as the short journey progressed, they began to second guess their initial assessment. The teenager's demeanor just seemed wrong. For someone who had just lived through the trauma of finding his entire family murdered, he did not appear to be distressed at all. In fact, he seemed excited, chattering away about how fast he'd driven his father's truck from the farm to the police station. At one point, he even asked the police officers what steps he needed to take to inherit his father's property. Deon Steenkamp owned several sheep farms in the area, and his estate was said to be worth millions. The officers told Don that he'd have to speak to his father's lawyers about it.

Their suspicions had been roused, though, and would only be heightened when they reached the farm and examined the crime scene. Deon Steenkamp, his wife, Christel, and 14-year-old daughter, Marthella, were dead, their bodies clustered together in the living room. They had each been shot twice, in the head and in the chest. The murder weapons were still at the scene. Don told the officers that he had found them near the farm gate. They were a .22-caliber hunting rifle and a .357 revolver, both of them registered to Deon Steenkamp. To the police, this was another red flag. Farm attackers usually arrive heavily armed with automatic weapons. They seldom, if ever, discard firearms. These are far too valuable and fetch a good price on the black market.

For now, though, the police filed that piece of information away and asked Don to explain how he alone had survived the attack. He eagerly did so, explaining that he had been doing chores in the barn when he'd heard gunshots coming from the main house, some 50 yards away. Afraid, he'd cowered in the dark until the shooting stopped, then waited a while longer before daring to emerge from hiding. He'd then approached the farmhouse, moving cautiously since he was afraid that whoever had fired the shots might still be around. They weren't. As he entered the living room, he saw his parents and sister lying on the floor. His mother and father were already dead, but Marthella was still alive, if only barely. He sat down on the floor and cradled her head in his lap until she breathed her last. That was how he'd gotten blood on his clothes. Realizing that his sister was gone and that there was nothing that he could do for her, he'd then taken his father's truck and raced into town to inform the police.

Don Steenkamp's story was far from convincing. Nonetheless, it was difficult to disprove, and the police had to keep an open mind. Perhaps it really had happened the way the boy said. Over the week that followed, detectives approached their investigation from two angles, investigating it as a possible farm attack but also as something more mundane, a family dispute that had ended in murder. It soon became evident that the latter was more likely. Farm attacks are characterized by extreme violence – the victims are tortured, the women almost always raped, the victims sometimes made to beg for their lives before they are killed. The killers then ransack the property, stealing money, firearms and anything else they can lay their hands on. Working in isolated locations with little to no prospect of a police response, they are in no hurry, often spending hours at the scene.

The Steenkamp murders did not match this modus operandi. According to Don's version of events, the attack had lasted mere minutes. The victims had not been tortured, and while an autopsy would later reveal that Marthella had been raped, Christel had not. The police also found it strange that Marthella was fully clothed. Whoever had sexually assaulted her had dressed her afterwards. This also did not tally with a farm attack, where female victims are often displayed for maximum shock value. And even if the killers had for some reason forsaken their usual barbarism in this case, why had they not ransacked the house. Nothing was misplaced, nothing but the firearms taken (only to be discarded later). Even the R60,000 (around $4,000) that Deon Steenkamp kept in his safe was still there. None of this made sense if this had indeed been a farm attack.

The other theory, that of some personal motive, had far more traction. Deon Steenkamp was well-known and well-respected in Griekwastad. A deacon in the local Dutch Reformed church, he was described as "a good Christian," generous and kind-hearted. He and his wife were said to live for their children. But Deon did appear to have anger issues. Farm workers gave him a wide berth when he was in a bad mood. Then anyone in the vicinity might fall foul of his caustic tongue, even his wife and children. All in all, though, he was considered a good employer who paid better than other farmers in the area and treated his workers well.

But while Deon was well thought of in town, the same could not be said for his son. The teenager was known to be arrogant, with a pronounced cruel streak. A farm worker had once seen him shoot one of his father's prized sheep dogs after she nipped at a puppy. He was also suspected of poisoning dozens of dogs in the town and made little effort to deny culpability. According to him, he was justified in killing the animals, since they were being used by locals to track and steal his father's sheep.

Was it such a stretch to imagine that the arrogant, entitled teen and his hotheaded father might have gotten into an argument, one that turned deadly and ended in the deaths of three people? The police did not think that it was a stretch at all, and the ballistics and forensics backed them up. Within two weeks of the murders, Don Steenkamp was in custody, charged with three counts of murder and with the rape of his sister.

Brought to trial in June 2014, Don Steenkamp denied the charges against him. He would continue to do so, even as the evidence painted him into a corner. Found guilty on all charges, he was sentenced to three terms of 20 years for the murders, plus an additional 12 years for rape. The sentences will run concurrently, meaning an effective 20 years behind bars. With time off for good behavior, he could be out in ten.

Heather D'Aoust

Jim and Rebecca D'Aoust were living the dream. Financially successful, the middle-aged couple lived in a comfortable home in the affluent San Diego suburb of Scripps Ranch. They shared that home with three teenaged daughters, Kimberly, Julie, and Heather, all of them adopted as infants. The family was happy, healthy, all-American. Jim and Becky loved the girls as their own and were rightly proud of their adopted daughters' achievements.

But there was one dark cloud on the D'Aousts' sunny horizon. While the two older girls had grown to be well-adjusted young women, 14-year-old Heather was a problem child. Undoubtedly bright, Heather was nonetheless inclined to surly, aggressive, and hostile behavior. She enjoyed testing boundaries. At times, she even pushed the infinitely patient Jim and Becky to their limits. She was also prone to self-harm, her arms marked by the numerous cuts she inflicted on herself. And she was a problem at school, too. Recently, she'd been expelled from the exclusive Christian college for propositioning another girl for sex.

For Jim and Becky, Heather was a difficult conundrum to solve.
Although they were determined to help their daughter, getting through
to Heather could be a challenge. Perhaps this was a product of the
genes she'd inherited. Both of her biological parents had suffered from
mental problems – schizophrenia and bi-polar disorder respectively.
Was it any wonder then that Heather was acting out? After discussing
the issue, Jim and Becky decided to refer her to a specialist.

An appointment was thus set up at the psychiatric unit of a local
hospital. Aware that Heather would likely refuse to go, Jim had
literally to trick her into accompanying him. By the time she figured
out their destination, it was too late to back out. Although angry,
Heather reluctantly submitted to the barrage of tests. The outcome of
those tests was as Jim and Becky had suspected. Heather showed signs
of bipolar disorder and was also suffering from depression.
Fortunately, these are conditions that can be controlled with
medication. Doctors assured the concerned parents that Heather could
live a normal, fulfilled life… as long as she took her pills.

The problem was that Heather refused to take the medication, sparking
a renewed series of rows with her parents, especially with Rebecca.
Heather resented the fact that she had been tricked into seeing the
doctor. In her mind, her parents only wanted her to take the pills so
that they could turn her into a "mindless zombie" who they could
easily control. She dismissed their assurances that they only wanted
what was best for her.

In fact, Heather had by now decided that the only way out of her
current situation was to murder the people who had raised and
nurtured her. Over the weeks that followed, she frequently ranted to

friends about clubbing her mother to death with a baseball bat. None of them took her seriously. They had all heard Heather's outbursts before.

But they might have felt differently had they been privy to Heather's internet activity. Among the terms she was searching at this time were "children who murder their parents," "kids who kill," and "evil children." Heather was doing more than making empty threats. She was thinking seriously about acting on her violent impulses. All that it would take was one spark to set her off. It came on the afternoon of May 24, 2008. That was the day that Becky returned early from work, entered her 14-year-old daughter's bedroom and caught Heather engaged in a sex act with one of her girlfriends.

Becky, of course, ejected the girl from the house and thereafter reprimanded Heather for her behavior. That sparked a huge fight between mother and daughter and led to Heather spending the rest of the afternoon sulking in her room. She did not even come down for dinner. By later that evening, though, the teen seemed to have calmed down. She even joined Becky on the couch to watch some television and seemed surprisingly affable. Neither she nor her mother brought up the earlier argument, and they spent a pleasant hour together. Becky probably thought that things had been resolved between them, but she was wrong. Inside, Heather was seething.

At around 4 a.m. on the morning of May 25, 2008, Heather D'Aoust got out of bed, put on a hoodie over her pajamas and headed downstairs, picking up an aluminum baseball bat on her way out of her bedroom. She walked out into the back garden, to an old tree stump, and started swinging the bat, crashing it repeatedly against the bark.

But this wasn't working for her. The bat was unwieldy. She needed
something that she could conceal, a hammer perhaps. She found one
hanging from the tool rack in the garage and stuffed it into the pouch
of her hoodie. Then she went to the kitchen and sat down on one of the
stools at the breakfast bar. The sun wasn't up yet, but that didn't
bother Heather. She could wait. She knew that Becky was always the
first to enter the kitchen in the morning. Today, Heather would have a
surprise waiting for her.

It was just before 8 a.m. when Becky made her entrance, yawning,
dressed in her nightgown. She greeted her daughter and remarked that
she was up very early and that she looked tired. "Couldn't you sleep?"
she asked. Heather didn't reply, but she did respond when Becky
asked if she had taken her pills.

"I'm not taking them anymore," she said in a deadpan voice. Then,
before Becky could even voice a response, she was off the stool,
rounding the counter, homing in on her mother. Becky still had her
back turned when the first blow connected with her skull.

"What are you doing?" Becky screamed, before Heather struck her
again, spilling her to the floor. Then Heather was on her, swinging
wildly with the hammer, striking her again and again. Meanwhile, Jim
D'Aoust had been roused by the screams and came running towards
the kitchen. Barely able to comprehend what was happening, he
entered the fray, dragging Heather away from his wife, suffering a
blow from the hammer as a result. He nonetheless managed to pull
Heather away, to wrest the hammer from her grip and to pin her down.

"Kill me!" Heather was screaming. "Kill me!"

"Call 911!" Jim shouted to his daughter, Kimberly, who had just entered the room. "For God's sake, call the police!"

Rebecca D'Aoust was still alive when police and paramedics arrived a short while later. She was rushed to a nearby hospital where doctors fought a desperate battle to save her life. However, the wounds were severe and would ultimately prove fatal. Within 24 hours of the attack, Becky was dead. Fourteen-year-old Heather was now looking at a charge of murder.

Heather, though, would not face her ordeal alone. She had one staunch, and perhaps surprising, supporter. Jim D'Aoust had just lost his wife of 30 years. He did not want to lose his daughter as well. "Heather's not evil," he told reporters. "She suffers from mental problems that she likely inherited from her biological parents."

Jim would pay all of his daughter's legal fees and would stand by her throughout the trial, even making an impassioned appeal for leniency during the sentencing phase. Tried as an adult, Heather was looking at life in prison without parole before she struck a deal with prosecutors and agreed to enter a guilty plea to second-degree murder. In January 2010, she was sentenced to 16 years to life. The first two years of that sentence would be served at a juvenile detention facility in Ventura County.

In 2012, the now 18-year-old Heather D'Aoust was transferred to the adult corrections system. Heather will be 30 years of age when she becomes eligible for parole. James D'Aoust continues to visit his daughter in prison.

Sean Pica

What would you do if a friend came to you and desperately asked for a favor? Would you help? Chances are that you would. Now imagine that you are a high school student, the friend is your classmate, and the favor she wants is the murder of her father. Still willing to help? What if she tells you that her father has been sexually abusing her since she was eleven years old? This was exactly the dilemma that 16-year-old Sean Pica faced in the winter of 1985.

The friend in question was named Cheryl Pierson. She and Sean had both grown up in Selden, New York, and had attended school together since kindergarten. Because their surnames were close alphabetically, they were often seated together, and thus a friendship was built up over time. By 1985, they were juniors at Newfield High, home room classmates, and close confidants who felt that they could discuss just about anything with each other. Well, almost anything. What Sean didn't know was that his friend Cheryl was hiding a dreadful secret.

Cheryl Pierson had been raised in a fairly typical American household. Her father, James, was a successful electrical contractor; her mother, Cathleen, was a homemaker. Cheryl had an older brother, Jimmy, and a younger sister, JoAnn. She did well at school, was popular with her peers, and was on the cheerleading squad. The family lived in a comfortable house at 293 Magnolia Drive. It was the very picture of suburban normality, but it was a lie. The Pierson family lived under the rule of a tyrant.

James Pierson was a strict disciplinarian whose word was law in his household. He placed stringent demands on his kids and forced them to abide by a draconian and always changing set of rules. Failure to comply usually brought swift and violent retribution. And the Pierson kids would have had it even harder but for the calming presence of their mother, who often intervened on their behalf. However, that was to change in 1979 when Cathleen fell ill and was diagnosed with a terminal kidney disease. Within a year, she was dead, throwing her husband and children into a turmoil of grief.

For Cheryl, just eleven years old at the time, her mother's death would bring even more dire consequences. During his wife's year-long illness, James Pierson had inexplicably turned his sexual attention toward his 11-year-old daughter. It had started with inappropriate touching, but it quickly escalated after Cathleen's death. Now Cheryl's only buffer was her older brother, James, but soon that layer of protection would also be removed. James and Jimmy were clashing ever more frequently, and eventually Jimmy moved out, leaving Cheryl and her six-year-old sister alone in the house with their father. The attacks became more frequent and more aggressive after that.

Cheryl was just 13 years old the first time her father raped her. Thereafter, the sexual assaults became a daily occurrence, sometimes several times a day. At first, Cheryl tried to fight him off, but she soon learned the folly of those actions. Eventually, she just gave in, allowed him to do what he wanted and prayed that it would be over quickly. Like most victims of incest, Cheryl Pierson carried a heavy burden of guilt over the abuse. She told no one, not even a boy she began dating at age 15, Robert Cuccio; not even the friend she could talk to about anything, Sean Pica.

But the veil of silence would not hold indefinitely. In mid-1985, Cheryl eventually broke down and told her boyfriend about the abuse. Robert initially wanted to confront James, but Cheryl begged him not to. He'd just deny everything, she said, and then the dirty secret would be out and she would have to bear the shame of it. By now, though, Cheryl had more to worry about than her reputation. JoAnn was nine years old, and Cheryl could already see how their father was looking at her. She was genuinely afraid that her little sister would become his next victim. Although she would not agree to Robert's plan of confronting her father, she did agree that something had to be done.

It is at this point that Sean Pica enters the picture. A few weeks earlier, Cheryl and Sean had been among a group of students who had been discussing a murder case that was all over the news at the time. A teacher at another Long Island school had paid one of her students $1,000 to murder her abusive husband. During the discussion, one of the group had asked: "Who would be crazy enough to kill someone for a thousand bucks?" Cheryl could still recall Sean Pica's response: "I'd do it for that amount," he'd quipped.

Had Sean been serious when he'd made this remark? Cheryl couldn't
be sure, but she nonetheless told Robert about it, and the two of them
agreed that she should raise the issue and see if Sean would be
interested in carrying out a hit on her father. That was how she came to
speak to Sean about the abuse she'd suffered at her father's hand and
how Sean agreed to be her hired gun for the fee that had been
mentioned before – $1,000.

But agreeing to kill a man, and actually following through with it, are
two entirely different things, as Sean Pica was soon to discover. A
former Boy Scout and the son of a New York police detective, Sean
was just not the type to commit a crime, let alone murder. As the
weeks and months passed, his resolve wavered, then dissolved almost
entirely. At the same time, he was plagued by guilt. A friend had come
to him with a problem and he'd agreed to help. How could he back out
now? How could he abandon her in her hour of need? How could he
allow her suffering to continue? Eventually, he decided that he could
not.

On the morning of February 5, 1985, Sean Pica rose early, dressed and
stepped out into the early morning chill. He was carrying a .22 rifle,
borrowed from a friend, as he left the house, making no effort to
conceal the weapon, and he started along the icy sidewalk. He was half
hoping that someone would spot him carrying the weapon and call the
cops. That way he would have at least tried to fulfill his obligation to
Cheryl and would have failed due to no fault of his own.

But no one spotted Sean along his route and no one tried to stop him.
Soon he was standing outside 293 Magnolia Drive with the rifle in his
hand. Then he was taking cover in the pre-dawn shadows and waiting

for his target to appear. When James Pierson emerged from his front door about a half-hour later, Sean simply stepped in front of him and raised the weapon. Not a word was spoken before he pulled the trigger five consecutive times, each bullet finding a mark in his victim's chest and head. Then Sean turned around and walked home, again making no attempt at concealing the weapon.

It was Cheryl, herself, who found her father's body, lying on its back in the driveway. Three months had passed since she'd hired Sean to carry out the hit, and she had resigned herself to the fact that he had backed out and wouldn't follow through. So, at first, she didn't make the connection. She'd later tell the police that she thought her dad had slipped on the ice and hit his head.

This was a murder committed on the spur of the moment. Still, Sean had been lucky. No one had seen him before or after, and no one had witnessed the shooting or even heard the shots. This lack of evidence led the police to believe, initially, that a professional hitman was involved. They even had a suspect, believing that Jimmy Pierson's ongoing feud with his father had finally come to a deadly conclusion. They would continue to hold that opinion until an anonymous tipster advised them to look at Cheryl Pierson and Robert Cuccio.

Cheryl and Robert were brought in for questioning and quickly wilted, admitting the entire murder plot and implicating Sean Pica as the shooter. Sean was then arrested and initially admitted to the murder, although his lawyer later convinced him to withdraw his confession. Sean had since discarded the murder weapon, and his lawyer believed that the state would have a hard time proving its case without it. He would be proven wrong in that assertion. Convicted of murder, Sean

Pica was sentenced to 24 years in prison, with the judge stating that it was his acceptance of the $1,000 bounty that sealed his fate.

The same could be said for Cheryl Pierson, of course. In her case, the court weighed up the long-term abuse she'd suffered and reduced the charge to manslaughter. Found guilty, she was sentenced to just six months and served only half of that time before being released. Robert Cuccio, who was given probation for his part in the murder plot, was waiting for Cheryl when she walked free. The couple later wed and remain married to this day.

But the greatest tale of redemption belongs to Sean Pica. While serving his sentence, Sean obtained his GED, then a Bachelor's degree, and then two Master's degrees in social work. After his release in 2002, he started working for Hudson Link, a program that helps inmates to further their education while incarcerated. He later became executive director of the organization.

Tim Kretschmer

On the morning of Wednesday, March 11, 2009, 17-year-old Tim Kretschmer dressed himself in black combat fatigues, armed himself with his father's 9mm Beretta pistol, and set off for the Albertville Realschule in Winnenden, Germany. The previous evening, the teen had posted a chilling warning in an internet chatroom he frequented. "I've had enough," he'd typed. "I'm fed up with this horrid life... always the same. People are laughing at me. No-one sees my potential. I am scared. I have weapons here and I will go to my former school tomorrow and then I will really do a grilling." No one who read the message took it seriously. Perhaps they should have.

Tim Kretschmer was a complex character. Born into a wealthy family on July 26, 1991, he was the older of two siblings. Somewhat of a mommy's boy, he grew to be a quiet, introverted child but nonetheless one who was prone to temper tantrums when he didn't get his own way. He did poorly at school and had few friends and not a single girlfriend growing up. His one real talent was table tennis which he hoped to pursue as a professional. But Kretschmer, while undoubtedly gifted, was most certainly not a team player. He often belittled and criticized teammates of lesser ability. In fact, his narcissistic behavior became such a problem that a coach eventually complained to his mother about it. As always, she sided with her son.

Kretschmer's other main interests in life had mainly to do with firearms. He was fascinated by guns and addicted to "shooter" video games. On most afternoons, he could be found in the woods behind his home, firing his air rifle, or hunched over a computer playing Counter-Strike or Far Cry 2. When not thus engaged, he would spend hours online searching for sadomasochistic material, particularly the kind that involved men being humiliated by women. His only social interaction was via chatrooms and a regular poker game that he and fellow students had at Café Tunix, a hangout popular with local teens.

If any of this suggests a young man beset by psychological problems, there were few outward signs. Neighbors described the Kretschmers as a normal, happy family who were well integrated into the community. The few friends that Tim did have said that he was an "ordinary kid with normal teenage problems." Nonetheless, Tim's anger issues were concerning enough for his parents to book him into the Weissenhoff Psychiatric Clinic in 2008. During his short stay, the boy met five times with a therapist and spoke openly about his growing anger and violent urges. The recommendation was that he should continue to be treated as an outpatient, but his parents failed to follow through on this. Despite a verified paper trail, they would later deny that he had ever been a patient at Weissenhoff.

In fact, Tim Kretschmer's parents appear to have been in denial about their son's mental state, dangerously so. In mid-February, he'd written them a letter, saying that he could no longer endure the suffering he was being subjected to. They'd put it down to teenage angst. That angst would soon result in one of the worst mass murders in German history.

We cannot say for sure what it was that finally tipped Tim Kretschmer over the edge. It has been suggested that he had spent the early morning of March 11 watching media coverage of a mass shooting in Alabama. Whatever the case, Kretschmer arrived at his former school that morning, armed and in combat gear. It was just before 9:30 when he entered the building and ascended the stairs to the upper floor. A short while later, students and teachers were startled by the sound of gunfire.

Kretschmer had entered two classrooms and a chemistry lab, opening fire on those inside. These were not wild, random shots. Krestchmer was an accomplished marksman, and he picked his targets carefully, going for headshots. By the time the school principal broadcast a coded message ordering a lockdown, nine students – Jacqueline Hahn, Stefanie Kleisch, Selina Marx, Viktorija Minasenko, Nicole Nalepa, Chantal Schill, Jana Schober, Kristina Strobel, and Ibrahim Halilaj – were dead. Also shot to death at the scene was a trainee teacher, Michaela Köhler. All but one of the victims was female. The shooter was clearly making a point.

By now, someone had called the police, and within three minutes of the first shots, officers had arrived at the school. Krestchmer, however, was not backing down. After a brief exchange of gunfire with the cops, he fled, killing two female teachers, Nina Mayer and Sabrina Schüle, along his escape route. He then exited the building, running along a road that passed a psychiatric hospital. Spotting gardener Franz Just on the lawn, he opened fire, hitting the 57-year-old and killing him instantly. Then, with police swarming into the area, he hijacked a delivery driver and ordered the man to drive him to the town of Wendlinger, some 25 miles away. With a gun to his head, the driver did as he was told. However, he saw an opportunity to escape just before they reached the Wendlinger on-ramp to the A8 autobahn. Spotting a police car parked on the grass verge, the man veered suddenly in its direction. He then slammed on the brakes, threw open the door, and bailed out of the van.

Kretschmer fled, too, running towards a nearby industrial estate. It was just after 12 p.m. when he entered a Volkswagen dealership with gun drawn. Brandishing the weapon, he demanded the keys to one of the vehicles from a salesman. The man complied, of course, but he had the presence of mind to drop the keys as he was handing them over. As Kretschmer stooped to pick them up, the salesman fled, leaving the building via a rear entrance. That escape, however, would have dire consequences for others in the showroom. In a fit of pique, Kretschmer opened up on salesman Denis Puljic and customer Sigurt Gustav Wilk, killing them both. By now, however, the dealership had been surrounded by police. Driving away was no longer an option. Tim Kretschmer was trapped.

But had Kretschmer ever planned on surviving his shooting spree? His next action would suggest not. At around 12:30, he emerged from the building and opened up on a passing vehicle, missing his target. Officers returned fire, striking Kretschmer in the legs, whereupon he hobbled back inside, crossed the showroom floor, and exited through the rear. An unmarked police car was stationed there, and Kretschmer fired at the occupants, injuring both men. He then made his way through the industrial park, shooting at anyone he encountered. Finally, with his injuries slowing him down and with police closing in, he sat down in an alleyway, put the pistol to his head and pulled the trigger. He had fired 112 rounds during his rampage, claiming fifteen victims, including himself.

The Winnenden shootings left the entire country in a state of shock. Such events are extremely rare in Germany. In its aftermath, many questions would be asked, many of them to do with the mindset of the killer and how his murderous intentions could have gone unnoticed. Of course, Tim Kretschmer could not have been clearer about what he intended, but it is easy to see why the warnings might have been ignored. It is easy to be wise after the event.

One question that was quickly resolved was the origin of the murder weapon. It was one of fifteen owned by Tim Kretschmer's father, a wealthy businessman and firearms enthusiast. The bulk of the arsenal was stored in a gun safe, but the Berretta was left unsecured in a bedside drawer where Tim had easy access to it. Multiple charges of criminal negligence would be brought against Kretschmer Sr. in the aftermath of the massacre. He was also required to relinquish his remaining guns. Regrettably, that would not undo the carnage that his son had wrought.

Jose Reyes

Jose Horacio Reyes Urtiz was born in Sparks, Nevada, on July 2, 2001. A second generation American, whose grandparents were from Mexico, he was the firstborn child of Jose Reyes and his wife, Liliana Urtiz. Jose Sr. worked in restaurants, first as a busboy, and later as a cook. When the economy slowed in the late 2000s, he moved his family, now expanded by two daughters, to Arizona. For a time, he worked in construction. But the restaurant business had always been his passion, and he'd always dreamt of owning his own business.

That dream was realized in 2011 when the Reyes family returned to Nevada and Jose opened Sparks Coffee Shop. The restaurant served breakfast and light meals and quickly became a popular eatery, with customers queuing to get in. This was in part due to the excellent food, in part due to the outstanding hospitality provided by the Reyes family. Jose Jr, by now a lively ten-year-old, was a familiar sight to customers. He spent his weekends, school vacations, and even some nights, washing dishes, greeting customers, and busing tables. Always cheery, always smiling, he was immensely popular with the regular patrons.

Few of them could have imagined what lay in the future of this charming little boy.

In fact, the seeds of destruction may already have been planted. From an early age, it was clear that all was not right with Jose. He was a slow developer who'd only spoken his first words at age five and had wrestled with speech and comprehension problems ever since. As a result, he struggled academically and was targeted by classmates who called him "stupid" or "retard." That usually provoked an angry (and perhaps justified) response, but there were also instances where Jose's anger was misdirected and inappropriate. He once threw a chair against a wall when he thought a classmate was mocking him for reading a book intended for a younger child. On other occasions, he grew frustrated and angry when he was unable to grasp something a teacher was trying to explain.

As the time approached for Jose to move from Agnes Risley Elementary School to Sparks Middle School, there were concerns about his ability to cope. At least one teacher red-flagged his immaturity. She recommended that he be sent for life skills training, but her request was turned down. Jose was allowed to graduate. It was at middle school that his problems really started to escalate.

Jose had been teased and taunted all of his life. Whether or not this was any worse than what the average kid suffers at school is difficult to ascertain, but one thing is certain, Jose took every jibe to heart, even those that were genuinely good natured. At Sparks Middle School, though, very little of it fell into that category. He was called 'stupid,' 'dummy,' 'retard,' 'gay'; he was jostled in the hallways and poked in the ribs; money was stolen from him. The most hurtful jibes came after he spilled water on his chinos and classmates joked that he had wet himself. Thereafter, he went by the cruel nickname 'pissy pants.'

Under the weight of this bullying, the once outgoing Jose retreated ever more into his shell. He spent more and more time in his room playing video games, his favorites being Grand Theft Auto, Assassins Creed and Call of Duty 4, all of them first-person shooter games. He was also scrawling furiously in a spiral-bound notebook, and those bile-filled outpourings would have terrified his parents if they'd known about them. So too would the internet searches he was conducting, "Columbine Massacre Role Playing Game" and "Top 10 evil children" among them.

But while those aspects of Jose's deteriorating mental state remained hidden, there were worrying signs that did not go unnoticed. In fact, Jose Reyes Sr. was concerned enough to book an appointment for his son with a psychotherapist. After listening to the boy's stories of bullying and teasing, the doctor concluded that he was suffering from depression and wrote him a prescription. That was on October 18, 2013. Just three days later, Jose Reyes would seek an alternative remedy for his problems.

Just after 7 a.m. on the morning of October 21, 2013, Jose's mother dropped him at school as usual. A short while later, just before 7:15, he was seen talking to a group of boys behind the school campus near the north hallway. Or perhaps ranting would be a better word. "Why are you people always making fun of me?" he yelled. "Why are you laughing at me?" For their part, the kids seemed to find it all quite amusing. The smiles were wiped from their faces, however, when Jose reached into his book bag and his hand came out holding a gun. He fired immediately, hitting one of the group in the shoulder. Then as the group (and other kids in the area) ran screaming towards the school building, Jose drew a bead on one of them. It would have been an easy shot but the boy didn't take it. Instead, he stalked off, heading towards the basketball court. It was there that he encountered math teacher, Michael Landsberry.

Landsberry was no stranger to gunfire. A former Marine, he had served two tours of duty in Afghanistan. He was also a member of the Nevada Army National Guard. A popular teacher who also coached basketball and soccer, he was affectionately known as Batman by his students, due to his love of the fictional superhero. Now, he approached the boy with the gun and demanded that he hand it over. Reyes, however, was not about to comply. "No!" he yelled as he raised the weapon. Then he fired, the bullet plowing into the teacher's chest. Landsberry crumpled to the ground, prompting one brave student to come running to his assistance. That was a mistake. Reyes took aim and pulled the trigger, hitting the boy in the abdomen.

And still, Reyes wasn't done. He continued stalking the grounds, taking potshots at any target that caught his eye. He then tried to enter the school building but found that the door had been locked. One can only speculate what carnage might have ensued had he gained access. In frustration, Reyes shot out a window. Then, with the sound of approaching sirens loud in his ears, he raised the gun to his temple and pulled the trigger.

Jose Reyes was dead, and so too was Michael Landsberry. The two other victims, both 12 years of age, were rushed to Renown Regional Medical Center for emergency surgery. Both would recover from their injuries. One of these boys, the first victim to be shot, was believed to be one of the kids who had frequently teased Jose Reyes.

There were still many questions to be answered, of course, most pertinently the source of the murder weapon. This was a Ruger 9mm pistol registered to Jose's father. It had been kept in a kitchen cupboard, out of sight but not otherwise secured. Both parents would swear that Jose was not even aware that his father owned the gun. They were quite obviously wrong in that assertion.

As for the motive for the shootings, that could not be any clearer. Jose Reyes had spelled it out in two suicide notes that he left in his infamous spiral-bound notebook. The first of these was directed at the students and teachers at his school. "You've called me gay, lazy, stupid, an idiot," he wrote. "You stole my money and accused me of wetting my pants. Well, that all ends. Today I will get revenge on the students and teachers for ruining my life. Have a great death at school." He had illustrated this note with a drawing of a tombstone. On it were the words "Sparks Middle School 1965-2013."

The second note was addressed to his parents and appeared to contradict the first. "This shooting is not because of the shooting games, bullying or other stuff," he wrote. "It is because of some bad things in the past because of me." He did not explain what these "bad things" were.

The note ended in poignant fashion. "And now I'm just a monster. If you hate me and my family doesn't love me it's okay. I know that I'm just an idiot. But I love you and I wish the past would be good and better someday."

Sarah Kolb & Cory Gregory

Adrianne Reynolds was a new kid in town and desperate to make friends. The pretty 16-year-old had recently moved from Kilgore, Texas, to East Moline, Illinois, to live with her biological father and her stepmother. She'd just enrolled at Black Hawk College in Rock Island County where she hoped to earn her GED so that she could realize her dream of joining the Marines. It was at Black Hawk that she met Sarah Kolb and Cory Gregory.

Sarah was one of the most popular girls in school; Cory was a hanger-on who was not-so-secretly in love with Sarah and followed her around like a puppy dog, even though she was dating another boy, Sean McKitrick. Soon Adrianne would fall in with this group, and a complex set of dynamics would surface. Sarah was bi-sexual and attracted to Adrianne. She hoped to have a relationship with her, but Adrianne was more interested in boys. This annoyed Sarah, especially when Adrianne took a liking to the sycophantic Cory. Sarah might not have been romantically inclined towards Cory, but she enjoyed having him around as a lackey. She wasn't going to let Adrianne interfere with that. Within a matter of weeks, these competing agendas had put the fledgling friendship under strain. Sarah was heard to utter several threats against Adrianne, including the threat that she was going to kill her. None of her classmates took her seriously.

And then, on the afternoon of January 21, 2005, there appeared to be a thawing of relations. That was the day that Sarah called Adrianne and invited her to lunch with her, Sean, and Cory at a local Taco Bell. Eager to patch things up, Adrianne agreed. She was waiting at the curb when Sarah and Cory arrived to pick her up.

We can't say for certain whether Sarah Kolb lured Adrianne Reynolds that day with the specific intention of killing her. We do know, however, that an argument broke out almost from the moment that Adrianne got into the vehicle. Right away, Sarah started accusing Adrianne of trying to steal her boyfriend. Adrianne snapped back that she wasn't interested in Sean, but that only seemed to feed Sarah's anger. By the time the vehicle rolled into the Taco Bell lot, it had gotten physical, with Sarah turned around in the passenger seat, tussling with Adrianne who was in the back. Several Taco Bell customers noticed some sort of commotion going on in the car, but none of them paid it much mind. They thought it was just teenagers goofing around. They could not have known that what they were witnessing was a murder.

Inside the car, Adrianne was gaining the upper hand over Sarah. A swing of her fist struck Sarah in the nose, causing it to bleed. But then Cory joined the fray, tipping the balance in his friend's favor. While he pinned Adrianne down, Sarah grabbed an ax handle that she kept in the car and started striking Adrianne in the face. Then she abandoned the weapon and got her hands around Adrianne's throat, tightening her grip and holding it in place until Adrianne's struggles ceased, until she went limp and there was no breath left in her body. As easily as that, a promising young life was snuffed out.

Adrianne Reynolds was dead, killed over a foolish, adolescent spat. But now her killers had a problem. What to do next? As they sat calmly in the car smoking cigarettes, they went over their options. Calling the police was out of the question. Even if they could convince the cops that the murder had been unintentional, they'd be looking at a long stretch in juvie. The only other option was to dispose of the corpse, and Sarah had an idea as to how that might be done. She instructed Cory to drive to a quiet spot where they could transfer the body from the backseat to the trunk. Then she directed him to her grandparents' farm near Aledo, Illinois. There, Adrianne's body was laid out on a tarp, doused with gasoline and set alight.

However, the juvenile killers would soon learn what many murderers before them already knew. A human body is extremely difficult to destroy with fire. The flames certainly blackened the corpse, seared off the hair, even cooked the flesh. But it did not consume the evidence of their misdeed. Eventually, after several hours, Sarah decided that burning wasn't going to work. A different strategy was called for. They were going to have to cut Adrianne up and disperse the body parts.

While this macabre drama was being played out, the Reynolds family was becoming increasingly concerned. Adrianne had been due to work a shift at Checker's restaurant that evening and had failed to show. That was not like her. When Tony Reynolds failed to reach his daughter by cell phone and when none of her friends could shed light on her whereabouts, Tony went to the police and reported her missing.

Adrianne's charred remains would remain out in the open, on a remote tract of farmland, overnight. But leaving her there was not an option, not if the killers wanted to get away with their crime. Sarah was making this point to Cory for the umpteenth time when he finally had a brainwave. He suggested that they call on Nathan Gaudet, a 15-year-old friend of his who had an unhealthy interest in blood and gore. Nathan was known to kill and dismember animals for kicks, so he'd probably have no problem with cutting up the body. He'd probably even enjoy it.

Sarah was initially reluctant to involve another person in the murder plot, but with little other option, she was forced to agree. And Cory's instincts about Nathan Gaudet proved accurate. The kid was positively elated at the prospect of carving up a human body. The following day, he accompanied Cory and Sarah back to the site, armed with his grandfather's handsaw. Adrianne was hacked into several pieces, her legs and torso tossed into a ravine, the rest of her unceremoniously dropped into a manhole at Black Hawk Historic Site.

Over the next few days, the police quizzed several of Adrianne's friends as to her possible whereabouts. Among those questioned were Sarah and Cory, and both of them denied knowing where she was. Sarah admitted seeing Adrianne on the day she went missing but said that she had given her a ride to a McDonald's and had dropped her there. She had not seen her since.

Had the conspirators stuck to that story, this would have been a difficult case for the police to solve. But, as is so often the case in these circumstances, there was a weak link. The enormity of what he had done had begun to weigh heavily on Cory Gregory. On January 30, one week after the murder, he broke down and confessed to his parents. Later that day, his father accompanied him to a police station, where he gave a full statement, admitting his role in the murder but naming Sarah Kolb as Adrianne's killer.

Things moved quickly after that. Sarah and Nathan were arrested; Adrianne's body was recovered; a bloody handsaw was handed over to the police by Nathan's grandfather; witnesses came forward to describe the struggle they'd seen in the Taco Bell parking lot. With his confession already on file, Cory Gregory entered a guilty plea at trial and was sentenced to 45 years in prison. Nathan Gaudet also pleaded guilty and was given five years juvenile detention for his part in disposing of the body. He was released in November 2008 and died three years later in an auto accident.

Which left Sarah Kolb. She entered a plea of not guilty at her February 2006 trial and raised a defense which sought to pin everything on Cory Gregory. According to Kolb, she'd had nothing to do with the murder and had only participated in the cover-up because Cory had threatened to kill her if she did not. All she needed was one juror to believe her story, and that is exactly what happened. With the jury deadlocked at 11 to 1, the judge had no option but to declare a mistrial.

But that would prove to be only a temporary reprieve for Sarah Kolb. In August that same year, a second jury rejected her protestations of innocence and found her guilty of murder and of disposing of a corpse.

Kolb was sentenced to 53 years in prison. She will be in her 70s by the time she walks free.

Rafael Solich

Rafael Solich was a strange kid. The 15-year-old, known as "Junior" to his family, was extremely introverted, with only one friend in the world, a boy of similar age named Dante Pena. At the Islas Malvinas Institute in Carmen de Patagones, Argentina, these two were given a wide berth by their classmates. It wasn't that they were aggressive or intimidating. They were just…weird. Rafael and Dante usually dressed all in black; they were obsessed with the music of Marilyn Manson; they claimed to be Satanists and were always drawing inverted crosses on school walls and lockers. They also conversed with each other solely in English so that their classmates couldn't understand what they were saying. This led others to speculate that they were plotting something, and they were both right and wrong in this assumption. Something was indeed being plotted, but Dante had no part in it. It was all Rafael.

There is little in Rafael Solich's background to warn us of the atrocity he would commit. Born in Carmen de Patagones, Buenos Aires Province, in 1989, Rafael was the older of two sons born to Rafael Solich Sr. and Esther Pangue. His father was a warrant officer with the Argentine Navy. His mother worked part time as a domestic servant. Rafael Solich Sr. was a keen soccer fan and sometimes took his son to watch Boca Juniors, the local Buenos Aires club. The boy's nickname, Junior, was a reference to this fandom. It suggests a close bond between father and son.

However, all might not have been as rosy as it seemed. In March of 2004, Rafael Sr. visited his son's school and spoke with the in-house psychologist. He said that he was having problems with Rafael at home, that the boy was violent and that he could not control him. He asked for help, and the school responded by referring Rafael for counseling. Ten sessions were ordered, but for some reason, the school failed to follow through and complete them. Had they done so, a disaster might well have been averted.

On the morning of Tuesday, September 28, 2004, when Esther had already left for her job and while Rafael Sr. was still asleep, Junior snuck into his father's room and took his service pistol and two spare magazines. These he stashed in his book bag. He then strapped a large hunting knife to his waist, concealing it under a black, military-style coat. With this in place, he left the apartment and headed for school. Islas Malvinas Institute was just a short walk away.

One of the attractions of the school (at least from the perspective of parents) was the strict discipline it maintained. The 400 students were required to attend a flag-raising ceremony each morning before heading to their respective classes. These began promptly at 7:35, and students were expected to be seated at their desks by 7:30, sitting in silence while they awaited the arrival of the teacher. On this day, however, one of the students was lagging. The class was already seated when Rafael Solich entered, dragging his feet in that odd gait that his classmates secretly mocked behind his back. Rafael did not head directly for his seat but stopped in front of the blackboard. It looked as though he wanted to say something, but instead he reached behind his back and began fidgeting with something in his rucksack. Then, at last, he spoke. "Today is going to be a nice day," he said, bringing his hand out in front of him. The children barely had time to register that he was holding a gun, when he started firing.

In the narrow confines of the classroom, with kids trapped behind their desks, it was a bloodbath. The gun that Solich was holding was a 9mm Browning Parabellum, a weapon with serious stopping power. It spewed death into the massed students. Evangelina Miranda was hit in the heart and died instantly; Federico Ponce was hit three times, once in the leg and twice in the chest. He too was killed. Sandra Núñez, another fifteen-year-old, died as a bullet plowed into her abdomen, destroying organs and blood vessels on its path. Five other children were also hit, suffering injuries of varying severity.

The carnage might have been even more devastating had Solich's weapon not clicked on an empty chamber. With panicked children now cowering behind desks and scrambling for safety, the shooter turned and walked from the classroom, reaching into his bag as he did so. He had two more magazines in there and the rest of the school still to cover. Slotting a magazine into the gun, he turned his sights on a member of the school catering staff who had come out into the corridor to investigate the ruckus. Solich fired but missed as the woman ducked through a doorway. It was then that Solich heard a familiar voice behind him.

"What have you done?" Dante Pena screamed at his friend. "Have you gone crazy?" Solich turned and spotted Dante just emerging from the classroom. Solich gave his friend a sheepish grin. For a moment, he seemed uncertain of what to do next, but then he started raising the gun. Dante might well have been shot had he not responded. Acting purely on instinct, he charged forward and plowed into Solich, tackling him to the ground. Then other boys emerged from the classroom and joined the fray. Between them, they were able to wrest the weapon from Solich and also to disarm him of the hunting knife he had strapped to his waist.

The Carmen de Patagones massacre was over almost as soon as it had started, but it had come at a terrible cost. Three children were dead at the scene. Five others were rushed to a local hospital where they would receive treatment for their injuries. All would eventually recover from their physical wounds. The psychological scars would take longer to heal.

In the meantime, Rafael Solich had been taken into custody and transferred to the port city of Bahía Blanca. There, he would be brought before a judge and would provide a bizarre motive for his actions, explaining that he'd been angry with his classmates since kindergarten and that he'd been planning an attack since the seventh grade. "They said I was strange," he whined. "They were always f**cking with me. Just because I have a pimple on my nose."

There was never any possibility that Rafael Solich would face murder charges. Under Argentine law, he was immune from prosecution because of his age. But there were serious questions regarding his mental health, and so he was placed in a psychiatric facility in La Plata where he would remain as an inpatient for the next three years. Eventually, in August 2007, the authorities began granting him furloughs, beginning with 24 hours per week and working up to 96 weekly hours. As of 2014, he has been more or less a free man, although he is still required to attend counseling sessions.

The Carmen de Patagones incident was the first recorded school shooting in Latin America. And it might have been so much worse but for the actions of Dante Pena, the undoubted hero of the piece. It was Dante who so bravely tackled and disarmed his friend. Had he not done so, Solich would have continued to rampage through the school. And with two fully loaded magazines and a hunting knife in his possession, who knows what carnage he might have caused. Dante, however, received no appreciation for his bravery. The opposite, in fact. Many in the community believed that he'd had prior knowledge of Solich's murderous plans. As a result, Dante and his family were ostracized. They eventually had to leave the area altogether, for fear of violent reprisals.

Brandon McInerney

This is a controversial case. It involves the issues of gender identity and sexual harassment, directly in opposition, one to the other; it involves two troubled boys, one 15, the other just 14 years old; it involves a school system that should have stepped in to avert a tragedy but didn't. Lest we forget, it also involves a tragic death and a life destroyed.

Lawrence "Larry" King was born on January 13, 1993, in Ventura, California, to a drug-addicted mother and a father who jumped ship before Larry was even born. By age two, he'd been surrendered to the child welfare authorities and placed up for adoption, which was how he ended up in the care of Greg and Dawn King. They did their best for their adopted son, but Larry was not an easy child to live with. As a toddler, he was diagnosed with attention deficit hyperactivity disorder (ADHD) and with reactive attachment disorder, a condition in which a child fails to develop relationships with his or her caregivers. Larry also struggled academically and was required to repeat the first grade. By third grade, he was showing distinctly effeminate characteristics, which saw him bullied by classmates. At just ten years of age, he announced to his stunned parents that he was gay.

And these were just the first of Larry's problems. At age 12, he was arrested for theft and vandalism and placed on probation. By November 2007, he had been removed from his adoptive parents and was living at a group home and treatment facility called Casa Pacifica. It was at this time that he started attending E.O. Green Junior High School. There he soon made his mark by showing up for school dressed in women's clothing, high heeled shoes, and makeup.

As can be imagined, Larry's flamboyant appearance made him a magnet for bullies, a target for schoolyard taunts. Far from being discouraged, though, he openly courted controversy. His behavior was over-the-top and often overstepped the mark into sexual harassment. He would frequently make sexually inappropriate comments to male students; he'd gawk at them while they were changing in gym class and comment on their anatomy; he'd even follow them into the bathroom and proposition them for sex, telling them to "just admit it, you know you want me."

The school authorities, it appears, were well aware of these behaviors. But even though some teachers felt that King's appearance violated the school's dress code, they were afraid to take action, afraid that they'd fall foul of California's strict gender discrimination laws. And in any case, Larry had a powerful ally in Assistant Principal Joy Epstein. Openly lesbian, Epstein was vocal in her support of Larry's right to express his sexual identity. She'd later be accused of encouraging his behavior to serve her own "political agenda."

Of all the boys that Larry King flirted with, of all the boys he taunted and harassed, there was one who he particularly singled out. He was 14-year-old Brandon McInerney, a kid who had endured a similarly difficult path through life to his tormentor. Brandon David McInerney was born on January 24, 1994, in Ventura, California. His mother, Kendra, was a methamphetamine addict with a record for petty crime. Brandon's father, William, also had a record. He had served time for domestic violence, including an incident in which he'd choked his wife unconscious. The couple eventually split in 2000, with Brandon remaining in the dubious care of his mother. Later, custody would transfer to William after Kendra entered a drug rehab program.

Just why it was that King homed in on Brandon McInerney is not known. What is known is that the pursuit was sustained and aggressive. It was also unwanted. King would often parade himself in front of McInerney when he spotted him in the school corridors. He'd shout out things like "I know you want me!" and "Love you, baby!" while McInerney stalked off in embarrassment. This would usually trigger roars of laughter from other students. It made McInerney a constant target for taunts and teasing, turning his school life into a daily grind. It was even beginning to impact his academic performance. And again, the authorities were well aware of this and did nothing. Deputy Principal Epstein apparently witnessed King's harassment of McInerney on more than one occasion. Yet, instead of reprimanding King, it was McInerney who she admonished, warning him over his "unacceptable behavior" when he became angry.

And then there was the incident which, in all likelihood, tipped Brandon McInerney over the edge. It happened during a school basketball game on February 11, 2008. In the midst of the action, Larry King walked out onto the court and asked Brandon McInerney to be his Valentine. That sparked a roar of laughter from the crowd as

McInerney made a rapid, red-faced exit. But King was not done yet. Later that day, he again made a public declaration of his love, this time in a school corridor. After that incident, McInerney tried to recruit several of his friends to ambush King and beat him up. But none of them was prepared to participate for fear of getting in trouble. That was likely when Brandon decided to take matters into his own hands.

The following morning, February 12, 2008, Brandon McInerney arrived at school carrying a .22-caliber revolver in his book bag. During first period, as Larry sat working at a computer, Brandon walked up behind him. Before anyone really understood what was happening, he drew the firearm, held it just inches from the back of Larry's head and pulled the trigger twice. Amidst the chaos of screaming, fleeing kids that ensued, he calmly dropped the gun and walked from the classroom. He was arrested a short while later, some five blocks from the school campus. King, meanwhile, was being transported to St. John's Regional Medical Center. He would die there, two days later. Brandon McInerney was now facing a charge of murder.

School shootings are, regrettably, an all too frequent feature of American life. But this one attracted more attention than most, mainly because of the high profile supporters that Larry King attracted, including Senator Hillary Clinton and talk show host Ellen DeGeneres. There were also marches and vigils by the LGBT community both in remembrance of Larry and to protest the victimization of its members. California politicians also got in on the act, with Assemblyman Mike Eng proposing a law that would make "diversity and tolerance training" mandatory in all schools.

In the midst of all this, there was Brandon McInerney. Brandon had his supporters, too, most notably among staff and students at E.O. Green Junior High School. A number of teachers acknowledged publicly that they had let him down, had failed to protect him from sustained and aggressive bullying. Other teachers pointed specifically to Assistant Principal Epstein as being culpable in this regard. Meanwhile, hundreds of E.O. Green students signed a petition, asking that Brandon be tried as a juvenile. With so much at stake politically, that was never going to happen.

On July 24, the Ventura County Superior Court ruled that Brandon McInerney would stand trial as an adult. On August 7, 2008, in the same court, McInerney pleaded not guilty to premeditated murder and to committing a hate crime. Later, after his first trial ended in a hung jury, he'd strike a deal with prosecutors, agreeing to enter a guilty plea to second-degree murder with the hate crime allegation dropped. Given the provocation he had endured in the run-up to the shooting, the sentence was a harsh one. Twenty-one years behind bars with no credit for time served and no possibility of parole until he has served his full term. Brandon McInerney will be in his late thirties before he tastes freedom again.

The true tragedy of the McInerney/King case is that it could have been so easily prevented. All it would have taken was for the faculty of E.O. Green Junior High to fulfill its duty of care to its students. It failed to do so, destroying two young lives in the process.

Jamie Rouse

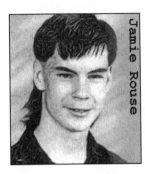

Afterward, after the crime scene tape was taken down and janitors were allowed in to mop up the dried blood from the hallways of Richland High School, the overriding question would be "why?" Why had this happened? Why had a seemingly normal high school senior taken a rifle and gunned down two teachers and a student? Why had no one spotted the warning signs?

In the case of Jamie Rouse, one does not have to dig too deep to find the answers. Jamie was a troubled kid, a teen subjected to frequent abuse by an alcoholic father, a kid who'd learned through hard experience to suppress his feelings of despair. His father, Elison Rouse, was a truck driver with anger issues and a liking for the bottle. When he was on the road, a tenuous peace would descend on the Rouse household, but once he got home, it was open warfare. Jamie, his mother, and his brother would be subjected to violence and verbal abuse. And they'd have to endure it without complaint. Crying around Elison Rouse was not a good thing. It only egged him on to greater cruelty.

And so the boy learned to bottle up his feelings and to express them in unproductive ways. He started drinking and doing drugs, he developed a taste for the most extreme death metal music, he became obsessed with the movie 'Natural Born Killers.' The film, starring Woody Harrelson and Juliette Lewis, is about a road trip undertaken by a serial killer and his psychopathic girlfriend. It is extremely violent. Jamie Rouse watched it over and over again. "I liked the way they made killing look easy and fun," he'd later admit. Perhaps that was what motivated him to pull a gun on his younger brother Jeremy during an argument. His father's response to this was surprisingly lenient. He simply locked Jamie's rifle away and told him that he wasn't allowed to use it for a couple of weeks.

While all of this was going on, Jamie was having trouble at school, too. From his earliest school days, he'd been a target for bullies, who picked on him for being "too quiet." Now, in high school, the other kids avoided him. The called him a Satanist due to his taste in music and his preference for dressing all in black. Many kids even professed to be afraid of him. On top of all that he was going through at home, it was difficult to take. Jamie felt isolated, ostracized. He felt like he didn't belong. This, as we have learned to our cost, is fertile ground in the making of a school shooter.

Still, it was going to take a spark to ignite the rage that was building in Jamie Rouse, and it came in the form of a poor report card. Now the put-upon teen really did feel like the whole world was against him. Not just his father, not just the kids at school, but his teachers, too, the very people who were supposed to be nurturing and guiding him. For Jamie, this was the last straw.

On the morning of Wednesday, November 19, 1997, 17-year-old Jamie Rouse drove his car to Richland High School in Lynnville, Tennessee. He was carrying with him a .22-calibre Remington Viper semi-automatic rifle, the same weapon that his father had recently confiscated. He also had several hundred rounds of ammunition. After parking in the still-empty lot, Jamie walked to a clump of bushes on the school grounds and hid the rifle and ammunition there. He then drove to the home of his friend, Stephen Abbott, who he'd arranged to pick up. He asked Abbott to drive as they headed back to the school. There, Abbott entered the building while Jamie skirted around, retrieved his rifle and then walked toward the north entrance. He had just stepped into the hallway when he spotted math teacher Carol Yancey in conversation with Carolyn Foster, who'd been a teacher at Richland for over 15 years. Without saying a word, Rouse raised the gun and fired.

The bullets were fired at close range, and Rouse was a good shot. The teachers never stood a chance. They were both hit in the head and fell to the ground. Then Rouse swung the weapon and brought it to bear on the school football coach who was standing nearby. But the coach was already on the move and Rouse's shot missed its mark. Unfortunately, it hit 14-year-old freshman Diane Collins in the throat, killing her on the spot. Rouse was then tackled to the ground by the football coach, who subdued and disarmed him. He was marched to the administrative office to await the arrival of the police who had already been called.

Given the amount of ammunition that Jamie Rouse was carrying that day, we should be thankful that his shooting spree was so quickly curtailed. Even so, the effects of what he'd done were devastating. Carolyn Foster was dead, and so too was Diane Collins, who happened to be the sister of Rouse's best friend. Carol Yancey was still alive but grievously injured with a bullet lodged in her brain. Against all the odds, she would survive the shooting and would ultimately make a full recovery.

But Jamie Rouse still had two counts of murder to answer for, and the bad news for Jamie was that the state intended putting him on trial as an adult. That meant that he faced the possibility of spending the rest of his life behind bars. Also arrested in connection with the shootings was Stephen Abbott, the boy who had driven Jamie to school that day. Abbott had been fully aware that his friend had a gun and 400 rounds of ammunition. He'd known what Rouse intended. He'd done nothing to stop the carnage. His complicity would ultimately earn him 40 years in prison.

Center stage, though, was the trial of Jamie Rouse who was facing one count of first-degree murder, one of second-degree murder, and one of attempted murder. Left with little other option, his defense team entered a plea of 'not guilty by reason of insanity,' claiming that Rouse was a paranoid schizophrenic who was not in control of his actions. According to his lawyer, Jamie had heard voices from God instructing him to carry out the school shooting. It was not a story that the jurors were willing to accept. They found Rouse guilty on all counts. He was sentenced to life in prison without parole.

These days, Jamie Rouse is an inmate of the medium security prison in Clifton, Tennessee. The prison sometimes receives groups of school kids from the surrounding towns, and on these occasions, Jamie Rouse is often asked to address them. "When I was 17 years old, I walked into Richland High School and shot two teachers and a student," he tells his audience. "Because of that, I'm in prison for the rest of my life and two people are dead. What I did, didn't have to happen."

One can only hope that the message sinks in with these impressionable youngsters. The problem of school shootings remains a scourge on the American education system and on society in general. Within four years of Jamie Rouse's curtailed shooting spree, we'd have the massacre at Columbine High. Other mass shootings have followed since then, with alarming regularity.

Nellie Corneilson

Contrary to what many believe, the phenomenon of homicidal children is not a recent development, not a symptom of the times we live in. These juvenile psychopaths have been with us throughout history. One only has to examine the murderous activities of the "Boy Fiend," Jesse Pomeroy, in 19th century Boston to verify that statement; or the even more extreme crimes committed by Cayetano Santos Godino, a 15-year-old serial killer who terrorized Buenos Aires, Argentina in the early part of the last century. Nellie Corneilson is not as well-known as the aforementioned killers, but the crime she committed is no less atrocious, more so because it was entirely without motive and perpetrated on a helpless child.

Nellie was born in 1891 in Madison County, Illinois, and spent the first eight years of her life there. In 1899, her father moved the family to Wichita, Kansas, in search of a better life. The Corneilsons moved into a house at the corner of Cleveland Avenue and Third Street, and Nellie started attending the Washington school where she excelled. She was a very bright girl who was way ahead of children her own age. In fact, her reading skills were equivalent to that of a 16-year-old.

Unusually for an eight-year-old, she was also interested in current affairs and studiously read the newspaper every day.

Two years into their stay in Wichita, Nellie's father moved the family to a new house at 1145 Dayton Avenue, West Side, a move that meant Nellie had to transfer to a new school. But the upheaval did nothing to dull the academic performance of this budding genius. The staff at the McCormick school found her every bit as bright as her former teachers had. She was also a diligent child who did not take her natural intellect for granted but worked hard to understand every new concept she encountered. Her teachers called her "a delight," which makes what happened next all the more difficult to comprehend.

Nellie had two siblings, a brother named Harvey, who was five years old at the time of our story, and a sister, Laura, just three years of age. The children were close and Nellie was particularly fond of her sister and often entertained the little girl. A favorite pastime was to play hide-and-seek in the barn that stood on their property. They were doing just that on the brisk afternoon of January 14, 1902, overseen by their mother who was standing at the back door of the house talking to a neighbor, Ada Baucher. At one point during the game, Nellie left the barn and walked to the house, passing her mother and Ms. Baucher without saying a word. A short while later, she re-emerged and headed back to the barn. The two adults saw her enter the building. Then, after a period of some minutes, she came running back out, screaming at the top of her voice. "Mama! A man hurt Laura!"

It was Ada Baucher who reacted first, sprinting towards the barn where she found little Laura lying on the ground, drenched in blood, a fountain of the stuff spurting from a wound to her neck. She immediately picked the child up, but then Mrs. Corneilson entered and snatched Laura away from her. Together, the women ran to the well where Ada pumped water and Mrs. Corneilson washed away the blood from Laura's neck. It was then that they saw the horrific extent of the wound, a straight cut that had sliced through the windpipe and the surrounding blood vessels. Mrs. Corneilson then screamed for Ada to call the doctor, and she ran back to the house to do so. By the time she'd made the call and returned, another neighbor had arrived with a buggy. Laura was then loaded into the carriage and rushed to the local hospital. She was still alive when she arrived. However, the wound ran deep and she had lost a lot of blood. She died later that night.

By now, the police had already begun their investigation, starting with an interrogation of Nellie. She, after all, had seen the attacker. Asked to describe the man, Nellie offered a rather vague depiction, saying that he was young and that he had been wearing gray clothes. Pressed for more details, she suddenly changed her story, saying that it was her brother Harvey who had cut Laura. Except that the police knew that wasn't true. Both Ada Baucher and Mrs. Corneilson had reported that Harvey had been playing outside the barn when the attack occurred. It was at this point that the police decided to bring Nellie to the police station for further questioning.

But Nellie would not be easily broken. Despite the best efforts of the police officers, she steadfastly maintained that it was Harvey who had cut her sister's throat. She had now expanded on her story. According to Nellie, Harvey had been playing "shave" with Laura, pretending to shave her with a piece of tin. He had probably misjudged the closeness of the edge and cut the little girl's throat by accident, she theorized. This, too, was a lie. The police had found the murder weapon, a bloody straight-razor, hidden behind a bale of hay in the barn. The blade had two distinctive nicks, and Laura's father confirmed that it was his. The police theory was that Nellie had been playing with her sister and had been overcome by some inexplicable instinct to harm her. She had then gone into the house to fetch the razor before returning to the barn to carry out the dreadful deed.

This theory was hardly a stretch. Indeed, it was the only way that the murder could have happened. But still, Nellie protested her innocence, still she continued to blame Harvey. Eventually, the officers decided to try a different tack. They took Nellie in to see her mother who was in shock and lying down on a cot in an adjacent room. The move had the desired effect. The minute she saw her mother, Nellie started crying. Then she ran to her mother's side, buried her face in her chest and sobbed, "Oh, Mamma, I did kill Laura. It was me. I cut her throat with the razor. I am so sorry."

"Why, Nellie?" Mrs. Corneilson wept. "Why did you do it?"

"I just did it, Mamma," was Nellie's answer. "I don't know why."

And that was the only answer that anyone would ever get out of Nellie Corneilson. This was a motiveless crime, although that did not stop people speculating as to the "real reason." One popular theory was that Nellie, the voracious reader, had read about a murder somewhere in a book and had decided to try her hand at it. A less outlandish idea was that Nellie had been mistreated by her father and had struck back at Laura, who was his favorite. There was never any evidence to back up either of these assertions. We are left with no reasonable explanation for Nellie's tragic act of fratricide.

So what happened to Nellie Corneilson? There is some ambiguity as to
her fate. Some reports suggest that she faced no repercussions for the
murder and was adopted by an uncle, who raised her on his farm and
kept her isolated from other children and from society in general.
Another version states that she was confined to a reformatory for girls
in Beloit, Wisconsin, remaining there for at least five years before
being released. Either way, she disappears from the history books
thereafter. We have no record of what happened to her in later life.

Nellie's murder of her sister did have one other victim, albeit an
unintended one. Her mother had been pregnant at the time, but the
child would be stillborn, leading many to speculate that the shock of
Laura's murder was behind the baby's death. He was laid to rest
beside his sister.

Rickie & Danny Preddie

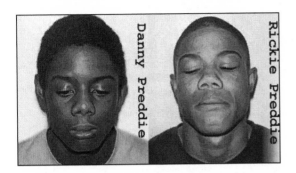

They were known to the police in Peckham, south London, as ruthless criminals. They were members of a gang called the Younger Younger Peckham Boys (YYPD), whose activities included violent street crime, burglary, and the theft of mobile phones, cash, shoes, leather jackets, anything of value. If there was a robbery in the Peckham area during the early 2000s, the police immediately suspected the Preddie brothers. At the time, Rickie Preddie was thirteen years old, his brother Danny just twelve.

And so, when 10-year-old Damilola Taylor was found unconscious and bleeding from a serious leg wound on November 27, 2000, the Preddies immediately came under suspicion. Damilola was a native of Nigeria who had moved with his family to the United Kingdom just four months earlier. He had started attending school there and was known to staff and classmates as a lively, intelligent boy who wore a perpetual smile and made friends easily. He was also a responsible child who walked himself to and from school every day, a journey that took him through YYPB territory. This had already brought him into contact with gang members who had jostled him and demanded money on a number of occasions.

Damilola usually spent his afternoons at an after-school club at the Peckham Public Library on Blakes Road, and he did so on the day in question. He was caught on CCTV leaving the library at 4:51 that day, and then heading down Blakes Road in what would be the final moments of his life. Thirty minutes later, a passerby found him lying in a pool of blood in a stairwell at the North Peckham housing estate. Unconscious and barely breathing, he was rushed to a nearby hospital. He didn't make it. A deep gash to his leg had severed an artery, causing Damilola to bleed to death. The little boy who had once written that it was his destiny to travel far and wide and remold the world, was dead, ten days shy of his 11ᵗʰ birthday.

But how had Damilola died? Although it seemed obvious that he had been attacked and stabbed in the leg, crime scene analysts offered another possibility – that his death might have been accidental. A theory was put forward that the boy had fallen and landed on a broken bottle which had severed an artery. The officers who worked the Peckham beat didn't buy that for a minute. They were well aware of how local thugs dealt with victims who resisted them. They employed a method of retribution that they called "juking." This involved stabbing the victim in the legs, sometimes with a knife but more often with a shard of glass or a broken bottle. Local officers were certain that Damilola's death was the work of the Younger Younger Peckham Boys. In no time at all, eleven members of the gang had been rounded up, the Preddie brothers among them.

The Preddies, however, had an alibi. Instead, four other members of the gang were arrested and charged with murder. These four youths were put on trial at the Old Bailey in 2002. There, the prosecution based much of its case on the testimony of an eyewitness, a 14-year-old girl who swore that she had seen the youths pushing and jostling Damilola shortly before he died. The defense, meanwhile, argued that there had been no attack at all. It cited the opinion of certain crime scene experts that Damilola had fallen and landed on a broken bottle. And it was this opinion that held sway. With the prosecution's key witness proving to be wholly unreliable on the stand, the defendants were acquitted. It appeared, at this stage, that Damilola's killers would go unpunished.

However, the police were not about to give up on the case just yet. During the initial inquiry, several items of clothing had been taken from the YYPB gang members and booked into evidence. By 2005, DNA technology had advanced sufficiently for those items to be tested. The results were telling. The Preddie brothers had sworn that they had been nowhere near the crime scene on the day that Damilola Taylor died. How then had Damilola's blood ended up on Danny's sneakers and on Rickie's sweatshirt? Blood was also found on the clothing of a third gang member, Hassan Jihad, who had been 14 on the day of the murder. Now the gang members, Jihad and the Preddie brothers, found themselves under arrest and charged with murder.

Five years had passed since the killing of Damilola Taylor, and the Preddies had not been idle during that time. They had racked up countless arrests for offences that included an indecent assault on two girls aged just ten and twelve. There were also arrests for robbery; for racially-aggravated assault; for burglary; for malicious damage to property; for making threats; for carrying a concealed weapon; for possession of cannabis. The brothers had also expanded their horizons.

They were now riding the London subway system and robbing commuters at knifepoint, threatening to slash their faces unless they handed over cash and valuables. As one police officer who was familiar with the brothers commented, "They were the scum of the earth." Getting them off the streets would likely result in a dramatic decrease in Peckham's crime rate.

But this would not be the slam dunk case that prosecutors believed it would. Despite evidence that the Preddies had previously assaulted Damilola at the very spot where he was eventually found, the jury failed to reach consensus. A mistrial was declared for the Preddie brothers, and there was an even more favorable result for Hassan Jihad. He was acquitted outright.

In June 2006, the Crown Prosecution Services again brought charges against Danny and Rickie Preddie, this time for manslaughter. A key feature of the previous trial had been the testimony of Alastair Wilson, associate clinical director at the Royal London Hospital and one of Britain's top trauma experts. Wilson had supported the theory that Damilola had died after falling on a shard of glass, and his testimony had been extremely damaging to the prosecution case. This time, the CPS was better prepared to offer a rebuttal. After 33 days of evidence, the brothers were eventually found guilty of manslaughter.

The sentences, however, were disappointingly lenient. Because of their ages at the time of the murder, the judge could impose a sentence of no more than eight years, to be served in a juvenile facility. And the Preddie brothers would not even serve out these exceedingly light sentences. Rickie was released in 2010, Danny in early 2011. They'd each served just four years for the brutal slaying of a little boy. Their release was met with outrage from the general public and fear by the people of Peckham. The Preddies were back on the streets. This could only end badly.

Danny, at least, seems to have learned some lessons from his time inside. He has mostly managed to stay out of trouble since regaining his freedom. For Rickie, though, it was business as usual. A condition of his parole was that he was not allowed to associate with known gang members, but Rickie simply ignored that. He was back in prison in March 2011 after he was seen hanging out with his former associates. Released in January 2012, he lasted just 16 days before he was again spotted with YYPB members. His next brief period of freedom ended when he stole a motorbike and then engaged in a high-speed chase with police. In November 2017, the now 30-year-old Rickie was again sent to prison, this time for driving offences and for failing to appear in court. As with the boy, so with the man, it seems.

Ronald Salazar

The warning signs were all there, clear as day for anyone who cared to see. Ronald Salazar was a danger to himself and others. The boy, just 14 years old, clearly held his family in a grip of terror. In fact, his father was so fearful of what Ronald might do that he asked the Florida State Department of Children & Families to intervene. That was in May 2005. According to Samuel Salazar, Ronald frequently threatened to kill himself and to harm members of his family. There were also concerns that he might be sexually abusing his sisters.

On July 13, 2005, a state social worker visited the Salazar home and heard testimony from Ronald's parents and siblings. Ronald, they said, was frequently angry, shouting, banging doors, and striking out at the merest hint of provocation. He'd once held a knife to his own chest and threatened to drive it into his heart. On other occasions, he'd attacked his siblings. His 12-year-old sister spoke of how he'd throttled her, leaving bruises on her throat.

And if the social worker believed that the Salazar family was exaggerating, she would soon have her own worrying encounter with Ronald to enter into evidence. The boy was in a belligerent mood. First, he admitted that he kept a knife under his pillow at all times. Then he threatened to use that same knife to slit her throat. As a result of this outburst, the teenager was ordered to be taken to a local hospital for psychiatric evaluation. However, the doctors there decided that there were no mental issues and that Ronald posed no threat to his family. This flawed diagnosis would soon come back to haunt them.

Less than two weeks later, on the morning of July 25, Samuel Salazar drove his 8-year-old son and 12-year-old daughter to school, leaving Ronald alone in the house with his 11-year-old sister, Marina. When he returned a short while later, he was surprised to find Ronald standing in a neighbor's yard. When the boy spotted his father, he immediately came rushing over, shouting, "We've been robbed! We've been robbed!" According to Ronald, he'd gone out into the backyard for a while and was still standing there when two black men emerged through the rear door of the Salazar residence and ran away. Ronald had been afraid to re-enter the house and had therefore gone to the neighbor and called the police from there. Samuel's next question was delivered with some trepidation. "Where's Marina?" he asked.

"I don't know," Ronald replied. "I think she's still in the house." It was at that moment that the police arrived.

But Samuel already felt a prickling of dread running up his spine. He did not believe a word of what Ronald had just told him. Something wasn't right here. In fact, something was dreadfully wrong. The officers had barely exited their vehicle when Samuel told them, "Grab my son. Don't let him go." One of the cops then told him to stand aside and he and his partner entered the residence. What they found inside would confirm the distraught father's darkest fears.

Marina Salazar was in her bedroom, lying under a 'Winnie the Pooh' comforter. She appeared to be asleep until one of the police officers peeled back the covers. He immediately let the comforter drop back into place. What he'd seen in that brief moment would stay with him for the rest of his life. The little girl's throat had been cut, the wound running so deep that the sheet underneath her was literally drenched in blood. An autopsy would later determine that Marina had first been throttled into submission before her killer had hacked into her neck, severing all the main blood vessels. She would have bled out in less than a minute. Further examination indicated that her vagina had been penetrated, with the rape occurring after death.

Who had committed this horrific crime? From the start, there was only one real suspect. Taken in for questioning, Ronald Salazar repeated his claim that he had gone out into the yard a short while after his father departed on the school run. He was still standing there when two black men suddenly burst through the back door and ran away. His assumption was that the men had entered through the front while he was in the yard and had probably ransacked the place. His initial thought was to go and check on his little sister, but he'd been too afraid, so he'd run to the neighbor to call 911.

Like Samuel Salazar, the investigators found Ronald's story difficult to swallow. They were almost certain that the teenager was responsible for the rape/murder himself. In fact, they were so sure that they did not even bother looking for the intruders Ronald claimed to have seen.

Instead, they increased the pressure on Salazar, and it wasn't long before he cracked and revealed the dreadful truth. It was he who had raped and murdered his sister. He and Marina had gotten into an argument, he said, and he'd then picked up the knife and attacked her. According to Ronald, he'd felt 'like a robot' while attacking Marina, as though it was someone else who was committing the atrocity.

Ronald Salazar was charged with first-degree murder. It would be four long years before the matter came before the courts, with Salazar facing trial as an adult and looking at a long prison term. Since he had already confessed to the murder, the main focus of the defense was to introduce facts in mitigation. There was plenty of material to draw on in Ronald Salazar's dysfunctional childhood.

Abandoned as a toddler, Ronald had been left behind in war-torn El Salvador while his parents fled to the United States. He had been raised in extreme poverty by his grandparents, who he'd believed to be his biological parents. That must have made it doubly difficult for him to understand the frequent sexual abuse he suffered at the hands of his grandfather. According to Salazar's later testimony, there was only one person who truly loved him – his grandmother. He was devastated when she died. Thereafter, he joined a violent street gang and got involved with drugs and petty crime. It was during this time that he discovered the truth about his parentage. While he was struggling to survive on the mean streets of San Miguel, his parents were living in apparent luxury in Miami. He also had a whole batch of siblings that he knew nothing about.

Ronald's parents did eventually do the right thing and bring him to Florida to live with them. However, the move was doomed from the start. The boy's childhood experiences had left him psychologically damaged. He felt unloved, displaced, a fish out of water. He was difficult, obnoxious, and frequently threatened violence against his parents and siblings. His father's response to this was to beat him and to abuse him verbally. In fact, the confrontations between father and son became so extreme that neighbors reported Samuel to the authorities.

Nothing had come of that complaint. Eventually Samuel had gone to the State Department of Children & Families and asked them to intervene before Ronald hurt someone. That report had resulted in Ronald's brief retention but he was soon released, thus sealing the fate of a sweet little girl, and condemning her to a horrible death.

In the end, Salazar's defense of 'not guilty by reason of insanity' was rejected by the jury. In October 2009, he was convicted on all counts and sentenced to two life terms. That sentence was later reduced on appeal to 40 years in prison. Ronald Salazar will be in his 50s by the time he walks free.

Jennifer Tombs

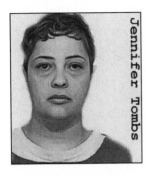

Jennifer Tombs was a problem child, and that was a constant source of embarrassment for her mother. Madlyn Tombs was pastor of the First Christian Assembly Church in Montbello, a suburb of Denver, Colorado. Her daughter's shenanigans were a long way removed from the message that she taught from the pulpit on Sundays.

At the tender age of 16, Jennifer had already racked up two juvenile convictions for aggravated car theft, with a third case pending. She had also been arrested for arson, after lighting her bed on fire. Then she'd violated the terms of her probation and had been ordered to wear an electronic monitor. One more transgression and the wayward teen would likely be sent to juvenile detention. That was a humiliation that the Reverend Tombs was not prepared to countenance.

But, in late September 1996, the reverend had a problem. She was due to go out of town on a church retreat, leaving Jennifer home alone. She shuddered to think what her daughter might get up to in her absence.

In fact, she was so afraid of the consequences that she was ready to call off her trip.

Fortunately, a member of Reverend Tombs's congregation had a solution. Errol and Valeria Vermont were friends and neighbors of the Tombs family, and Errol was an associate pastor at First Christian Assembly. He suggested that his stepdaughter, 23-year-old Latanya Lavallais, could move into the reverend's house while she was out of town. That would allow her to keep an eye on Jennifer. Since the reverend knew Latanya to be a responsible and level-headed young woman, she readily agreed. Latanya and Jennifer were close, but Reverend Tombs was confident that Latanya would keep her in line and out of trouble.

What the good reverend didn't know was that Jennifer was already involved in activities that would have seen her probation revoked on the spot, should the authorities have found out about them. The most serious of these was that she had obtained a firearm from her new boyfriend, Joaquin Johnson. Jennifer had told the naïve young man that she needed the gun to protect her baby from some men who had been harassing her. There was no baby, of course, but Johnson only found that out when it was already too late, when his .25-caliber pistol had been used to deadly effect.

For now, though, Reverend Tombs thanked the Vermonts for their generosity and provided Latanya with final instructions. Jennifer was not to leave the house and she was also not allowed to invite friends over. Reverend Tombs knew very well the kind of company her daughter kept. They were not the sort of people who belonged in a Christian home.

Reverend Tombs departed for her retreat on the afternoon of Friday, September 27, 1996. She was barely out the door when Jennifer started agitating with Latanya. She wanted to go out. When Latanya refused permission, the teenager changed tack, now begging her babysitter to allow her to invite some friends over. Since Latanya had been prepped for exactly this scenario, she refused. That, however, was not the end of the story. Jennifer continued to bait and harass Latanya for several hours, with the exchange becoming increasingly antagonistic. We know this because when Latanya spoke on the phone to a friend later that evening, Jennifer could be heard in the background, ranting and raving.

On the morning of Saturday, September 28, Denver police received a call from a young woman who identified herself as Jennifer Tombs and said that she had just found her babysitter shot to death. Officers raced to the address where they discovered Latanya Lavallais in the basement, shot five times in the back of the head. According to the story told by Tombs, she had snuck out of the house for an hour and had returned to find the place in darkness. She had assumed that Latanya had gone to sleep, and so she'd crept off to bed herself. It was only the next morning, when she couldn't find Latanya, that she realized something was wrong. It was then that she searched the house and found the young woman in the basement, shot to death.

The police were immediately suspicious of this story and became even more so when they interviewed Jennifer's boyfriend, Joaquin Johnson. He told detectives that Jennifer had called him at around 4 a.m. that morning and told him that a female intruder had broken into the house during the night and that she had shot and killed her. Johnson also told the police about the weapon he'd given Jennifer. Asked about the gun, the 16-year-old insisted that she didn't have it. Whoever shot Latanya must have taken it, she said.

But the police would soon find the gun, in a drain just 200 feet from the Tombs residence. Confronted with this, Jennifer changed her story. She now admitted that she had shot Latanya but claimed that it had been an accident. According to this revised story, she had been awakened by a noise during the night. Thinking that there was an intruder in the house, she had taken the gun and gone down stairs. There she had been confronted by a figure that "came at her out of the dark." Spooked, she pulled the trigger and kept firing until the figure collapsed to the ground. It was only after she turned on the light that she realized that she'd shot Latanya. She'd then panicked and decided to cover up the crime.

This story also did not ring true with investigators. Latanya Lavallais had been shot five times in the back of the head, which did not gel with Jennifer's assertion that she'd "come at her." Detectives also could not believe that someone untrained in the use of a firearm could have hit a target five times out of five in a darkened room. Their explanation for the shooting was far simpler. Jennifer and Latanya had gotten into an argument over Latanya's refusal to let her invite her friends to the house. Things had become heated and, at some point, Jennifer had fetched the gun and used it to kill her babysitter. This version of events was backed up by the testimony of Jennifer's boyfriend and by the friend who had spoken to Latanya earlier in the evening.

Jennifer Tombs was arrested and charged with first-degree murder. But there was at least one person who believed in her innocence. The

Reverend Madlyn Tombs swore that her daughter had not done the thing that she was accused of and preached this message from the pulpit of her church, even while the victim's parents were sitting in the pews. As a result, the congregation turned on Errol and Valeria Vermont, who they considered to be making false accusations against their beloved pastor's daughter. Errol and Valeria were effectively driven from their church at the very time that they most needed the love and support of their fellow worshipers.

Jennifer Tombs went on trial in March 1997 with the congregation of the Montbello First Christian Assembly Church turning out in force to support her. That support would be to no avail, as she was found guilty of first-degree murder and sentenced to life without parole. A subsequent appeal was turned down, but the 2012 Supreme Court ruling on juvenile lifers gives Tombs hope that she might one day be released.

Andrew Williams

The story of Charles Andrew Williams is a tragedy, a tale of two young lives lost and another wasted; of a happy, promising young boy driven to murder by a toxic combination of drugs, bullying, and bad influences. It is an indictment on indifferent parenting and the American education system.

Charles Andrew Williams (known as "Andy" to friends and family) was born in Frederick, Maryland, on February 8, 1986, to Jeff and Linda Williams. A premature baby, delivered by C-section, he spent the first week of his life in the hospital before joining his parents and older brother at the family home. Later that year, his mom (who was serving in the US Army) was transferred to Fort Detrick, Maryland, where the family would spend the next two-and-a-half years, until June of 1989. That was when Linda was assigned to the Middle East, a posting that would lead to the breakdown of the Williams marriage. By December of that year, Jeff and Linda had decided to divorce. The split came in 1990, with older brother Michael going to live with their mother and Andy remaining with his father. He seldom saw his mother or sibling after that.

Raising a kid as a single parent is difficult, but Jeff Williams seemed
up to the task. He and Andy had a strong father/son bond, even if their
lifestyle was somewhat nomadic. Over the next few years, they'd
move from Frederick to Hagerstown, then back to Frederick and
finally to Knoxville, Maryland. Despite these disruptions, Andy did
well at school, was keen on sports, loved animals, and had plenty of
friends. He was known around his Knoxville neighborhood as a happy
and respectful youngster. At Brunswick Middle School, he was
running for Class President. Then, in 1999, disaster. His father told
him that they were moving to California.

Andy wasn't at all keen on the move west. But after arriving in the
small Californian town of Twentynine Palms, he quickly settled in. His
paternal grandparents lived close by, and he soon made friends at
Twentynine Palms Junior High School. He became interested in drama
and was chosen to play the role of Linus in the school production of
"You're a Good Man, Charlie Brown." He also became close friends
with a fellow student, Brian Burdette, a boy who suffered from a
crippling muscular disease and was frequently bullied. Then, just when
Andy was getting some stability back into his life, his father
announced that they were moving again, to the town of Santee, 175
miles to the southwest.

After the relaxed, friendly atmosphere of Twentynine Palms, Santee
would be a rude awakening for Andy. He was enrolled at Santana
High, a school with a good reputation but with an underlying gang
culture. Almost immediately, he became a target for bullies. He was
roughed up, punched and kicked in the corridors, burned with a lighter.
Things weren't all that great at home either. Bogged down with work
at his new job, Jeff Williams had become an absent parent. Even when

he was home, he was either hunched over his computer or sprawled out in front of the TV, drinking beer.

Left on his own and desperate to fit in, Andy started hanging out with a bunch of drugged-up skateboarders in nearby Woodglen Vista Park. That was how he was first introduced to drugs. Andy Williams, formerly an obedient, upstanding kid from Maryland, was now ditching school, getting wasted on dope and tequila, and shoplifting from the Albertson's supermarket across the road from his school. He was also joining in enthusiastically in a favorite topic of conversation among his new cohorts, the recent massacre at Columbine High School.

At Santana High, meanwhile, Andy continued to be a target for bullies. Even amongst his skater friends, he was sometimes the target for taunting and teasing. Perhaps that was why he first started talking about carrying out a school shooting of his own, his own Columbine, as he described it. "And how are you going to do that?" his friends teased, "You don't even have a gun."

"My dad has a whole collection in his safe," Andy replied defiantly. "I'll just steal one, and some ammo." That, at least, got their attention. That, at least, got them to shut up and listen. That got their respect, and Andy was desperate for someone to respect him, to take him seriously.

Over the weeks that followed, the group of friends continued to discuss Columbine and the potential of a similar shooting at their own school. And Andy soon realized that the currency of making threats only went so far. His friends had decided that he was all talk and no

action. They started taunting him again, telling him that he was
chicken and would never go through with it. They were somewhat less
dismissive when he showed up one day with a gun – a long-barreled
Arminius .22-caliber revolver – that he'd taken from his father's safe.
That shut them up alright. It also pushed Andy Williams further along
the path to murder.

Still, there is a long road between making threats of violence and
actually carrying out those threats. So what was it that finally pushed
Andy Williams over the edge? Most likely, it was not a single thing
but an accumulation of factors. Bullying certainly played a part, as did
the desperate need that Andy had for acceptance. A more involved
parenting style might have lessened the boy's feelings of isolation, but
Jeff Williams was occupied with his own life, locking Andy out. As in
many school shootings, music also played a part. Friends would later
say that Andy was heavily influenced by the lyrics of a Linkin Park
song, In the End. *"In spite of the way you were mocking me/ Acting
like I was part of your property/ Remembering all the times you fought
with me/ I'm surprised it got so far."*

And then there was the death of Andy's close friend from Twentynine
Palms, Brian Burdette. Burdette was killed in an auto accident in
February 2001. Andy, always a sensitive kid in spite of his newfound
rebelliousness, took it hard. Just a few weeks later, on the morning of
March 5, 2001, he would enter Santana High School carrying a loaded
gun.

It was just after 9:20 a.m. on that Monday that a volley of shots rang
out in the school halls. Many of the students thought that fireworks
were being let off as a prank and rushed in the direction of the sound.

But they soon backed off when they saw blood on the floor and their injured classmates trying to crawl away. Then the shooter emerged from a bathroom and fired off another volley, causing a panicked stampede of screaming kids.

Williams would repeat this action several times, emerging from cover, firing wildly down the corridor, and then slipping back into the bathroom. Between each volley, he reloaded the eight-shot revolver. Eventually, campus security supervisor Peter Ruiz decided to put an end to the siege and walked bravely, if foolhardily, into the bathroom. He ordered Williams to hand over the revolver, but Williams refused and backed him off with the gun. Then, as Ruiz turned to leave, Williams fired once, hitting him in the back. The security supervisor managed to scramble to safety and would later recover from his wound.

But not everyone was so lucky. Two students – 14-year-old Bryan Zuckor and 17-year-old Randy Gordon – were already dead. Thirteen others had suffered gunshot wounds of varying seriousness. Already, this was the worst school shooting since Columbine. Help, though, was at hand. The police had been summoned, and officers now arrived at the scene and stormed Williams's position. The shooter was taken into custody without a fight. When the police entered the bathroom, they found him kneeling on the tiled floor with the weapon in his hands. Ordered to surrender the firearm, he immediately complied.

Andy Williams was taken into custody that day and would remain in juvenile detention while a legal battle raged over whether he should be tried as an adult. That impasse was finally resolved when Williams decided to plead guilty to the charges of murder against him – two counts of murder, 14 of attempted murder. On June 20, 2002, he appeared in adult court and entered his pleas. He was then sentenced to 50 years in prison. He would be held in the Youth Offender Program at Tehachapi until his 18th birthday and then transferred to adult prison. Williams is currently incarcerated at Calipatria State prison. He has been a model inmate throughout his period of incarceration and has every expectation of being paroled at the first opportunity.

Jason Gamache

On the afternoon of Saturday, October 24, 1992, a group of children was playing hide-and-seek at a condominium complex in Courtenay, British Columbia. As the day began to fade to dusk, Carol Shaw, the mother of three of the kids, came out to call them in to dinner. Two of her children, 10-year-old Anthony and 4-year-old Robin, responded right away, but Dawn, the middle child at six years of age, did not. That sparked a search which grew ever more frantic as Carol failed to locate the little girl. Soon neighbors had joined in the effort. Then a couple of police officers, who were in the neighborhood on other business, took charge. When it became apparent that Dawn was not inside the complex, searchers were directed towards the adjacent school grounds and the woods beyond.

It was a neighbor, Lloyd Doucet, who found Dawn. The little girl's naked body was lying on the ground just beyond the tree line, at the convergence point of two paths. She had been left exposed to the elements, with no attempt at concealment. Her pale skin was covered in cuts and bruises, and mud was smeared on her chest. A muddy shoeprint with a diamond pattern was imprinted on her face, suggesting that she had been stomped. An autopsy would later conclude that she had suffered multiple fractures and had died of internal bleeding. She had also been raped.

Dawn Shaw's horrific death would send shock waves through Courtenay and across British Columbia. Determined to catch the killer, the Royal Canadian Mounted Police (RCMP) launched a massive investigation, one that zeroed in almost immediately on Dawn's 15-year-old neighbor, Jason Gamache. Standing 6'1'' and powerfully built, Gamache was more than capable of overpowering a little girl. Moreover, Dawn and her siblings knew him well. It would have been easy for him to lure her into the woods. And Jason had been seen playing hide-and-seek with the children on the day that Dawn was killed. That put him firmly in the frame.

There was a problem, though. Jason just did not seem the type. Everyone who the police spoke to described him as a pleasant, mature, and outgoing teen. He was said to have a real rapport with kids and was the go-to babysitter in the complex where he lived. In fact, Jason had been asked to take care of a group of children on the night that Dawn was killed. While the adults were out searching for the missing girl, it was Jason who was minding their children. No one believed that he would ever harm a child.

But Jason Gamache's neighbors were dangerously misinformed about the teenager. As the police started looking into Gamache's background, they discovered that he was a convicted sex offender. Two years earlier, in his home town of Nanaimo, Gamache had lured two four-year-olds, a boy and a girl, into his home and had asked them to perform oral sex on him. The boy had complied but the little girl

had refused and Gamache had let her go. She later told her mother
about the incident, which led to the matter being reported to the police.

Found guilty of sexual assault, Gamache had received no jail time but
was instead ordered to undergo treatment. And since the best resource
for such therapy was in Courtenay, his mother decided to move there.
She soon found a low-rent condo and moved in next door to the Shaw
family. Carol Shaw would have had no inkling of the sex offender
living in close proximity to her children, since Gamache's identity was
protected under Canada's Young Offenders Act. Now, though, his
dark past had been uncovered. He was firmly in the sights of RCMP
investigators.

But if the police thought that the 15-year-old would roll over the
minute they got him into an interrogation room and put the heat on
him, they were sorely mistaken. Gamache admitted that he'd been
playing hide-and-seek with the children that day but steadfastly denied
any involvement in Dawn's death. He even agreed to take a lie
detector test, which was administered two days later in Victoria,
Vancouver. He passed with flying colors.

The result of the polygraph was a setback to the police. Was it possible
that they had the wrong man? Might Gamache be innocent? After all,
he'd been asked on nine separate occasions during the test whether
he'd killed Dawn. Each time he'd answered no and the needle had
barely budged. Was it possible that someone else had killed Dawn
Shaw? And if so, who? The truth was that the police had no other
suspects. Everything now rested on the forensic tests that were being
conducted on Gamache's clothing, the black tracksuit and trainers he'd
been wearing on the day that Dawn died.

The speed at which forensic tests could be administered was considerably slower in the 90s than it is today. During the agonizingly slow weeks that detectives awaited the outcome, Gamache was at liberty, attending school and interacting with his neighbors, including the Shaw family. During that time, he appeared entirely calm. He even helped a neighbor make and distribute pink ribbons in Dawn's memory. Discussing the case with classmates, he admitted that the police had questioned him but insisted that they had the wrong man. He told the same story to his mother when she asked him outright whether he'd hurt Dawn. "Mom, I swear to you, it wasn't me." The tears glistening in his eyes made her believe that he was telling the truth. Or perhaps that was just what she wanted to believe.

In the end, the forensic evidence would make a liar of Jason Gamache. Fibers found on Dawn's discarded clothing were matched conclusively to black strands from Gamache's tracksuit and to red strands from a rug found in the living room of his apartment. The unique diamond pattern that had been noted on Dawn's face was an exact match to the tread of Gamache's sneakers. Brought down to the police station and confronted with these findings, Gamache finally broke down and admitted that he had killed the little girl.

Speaking in the presence of his mother, the juvenile killer calmly described the events of that horrific day. He said that he had lured Dawn into the woods by promising to show her a hiding place where the others would never find her. He'd carried her into the cover of the trees riding on his shoulders, he said. There, he forced her to undress and then sexually assaulted her. He said that he had planned to let her go after warning her not to tell anyone what had happened. But then he heard Dawn's brother, Anthony, calling for her and he "just lost control." He grabbed Dawn by the throat to prevent her calling out to her brother. Then he started throttling her, maintaining his grip until her eyes glazed over. He dropped her, then semi-conscious, onto the ground. Then he started jumping on her, by his own admission, "jumping up into the air and landing on her," snapping bones and destroying organs beneath his weight. Dawn's last word, according to Gamache, was "mommy."

Jason Gamache was arrested and charged with murder. It would take a year of legal argument before it was eventually decided that he would be tried as an adult. That meant, of course, that his identity could finally be revealed. At trial, Gamache was damned by his own videotaped confession. However, it had never been his intention to claim innocence. Rather, he entered a plea of "not guilty by reason of insanity." According to experts put forward by his legal team, he was suffering from multiple personality disorder. Jason had not committed the murder, his lawyer argued, it was his evil alter-ego, Karl. That spurious defense would ultimately fail.

Found guilty of first-degree murder in April 1994, Jason Gamache was sentenced to life in prison with no parole for ten years. He would serve just three years of that sentence. On February 3, 1997, the now 20-year-old Gamache was found hanging from a shower head at the Mountain Institution correctional facility. At first, it was thought that he had committed suicide. Later, it was determined that he had died while engaging in auto-erotic asphyxiation.

For more True Crime books by Robert Keller please visit

http://bit.ly/kellerbooks